A NEW FRAMEWORK FOR THE CARE
AND UPBRINGING OF CHILDREN

MANUAL
OF PRACTICE
GUIDANCE
FOR
GUARDIANS
AD LITEM
AND
REPORTING
OFFICERS

London: TSO

Published by TSO (The Stationery Office) and available from:

Online
www.tso.co.uk/bookshop

Mail, Telephone, Fax & E-mail
TSO
PO Box 29, Norwich, NR3 1GN
Telephone orders/General enquiries: 0870 600 5522
Fax orders: 0870 600 5533
E-mail: book.orders@tso.co.uk
Textphone 0870 240 3701

TSO Shops
123 Kingsway, London, WC2B 6PQ
020 7242 6393 Fax 020 7242 6394
68-69 Bull Street, Birmingham B4 6AD
0121 236 9696 Fax 0121 236 9699
9-21 Princess Street, Manchester M60 8AS
0161 834 7201 Fax 0161 833 0634
16 Arthur Street, Belfast BT1 4GD
028 9023 8451 Fax 028 9023 5401
18-19 High Street, Cardiff CF10 1PT
029 2039 5548 Fax 029 2038 4347
71 Lothian Road, Edinburgh EH3 9AZ
0870 606 5566 Fax 0870 606 5588

TSO Accredited Agents
(see Yellow Pages)

and through good booksellers

First published 1992
Second impression 2003

ISBN 0 11 321495 2

Prepared for the Department of Health
by Judith Timms, Director for IRCHIN

Independent Representation of Children in Need
Registered Charity No 326387

This manual could not have been completed without
the valuable contributions of many professionals
who have particular expertise in this complex field.

Printed in the United Kingdom for The Stationery Office
146481 C5 07/03 5673

Contents

A Manual of Practice Guidance for Guardians ad Litem and Reporting Officers

Foreword

The Children Act 1989, implemented on October 14th 1991, substantially enhances the role of the guardian ad litem in public law proceedings. Under the provisions of the Act, guardians ad litem will be appointed more often to safeguard the interests of the child in a wider range of proceedings in the Magistrates, County and High Courts. The function of the service is to provide independent social work advice to the courts, aimed at safeguarding and promoting the interests of the child in care, child protection, adoption and related court proceedings. In addition to the role of independent expert on behalf of the child, guardians will take on significant new case management functions. These include assisting the courts to take a pro-active stance, in order to avoid unnecessary delays, expediting proceedings and exploring the full range of possible orders and powers within the Act.

This Manual provides practice guidance to guardians ad litem and reporting officers who will be playing a critical and central role in the successful implementation of the Children Act 1989. However, all panel members should read, have copies of and be familiar with the Act, the Rules of Court and all the volumes of Guidance and Regulations and will wish to develop their own practice as they gain experience of the Act in action. In particular this manual should be read in conjuction with Volume 7 of the Guidance and Regulations "Guardians ad Litem and Other Court Related Issues".

PART I

THE LEGAL FRAMEWORK

Chapter 1

Introduction

The need for a guardian ad litem or an independent voice to speak for the child in care proceedings was first highlighted by the Committee of Inquiry into the death of Maria Colwell in 1974. The Report stated that "it would have been of assistance to the court to have had the views of an independent social worker"—"independent" in this case meaning independent of the local authority and of the child's parents. Solicitors had already become aware of the need for separate representation for the child and clause 42 of David Owen's 1974 Children Bill stated that "in any proceedings relating to a minor in any court, separate representation should be considered and, if appropriate, the child should be made (if not already so) a party to the proceedings". The Children Act 1975 incorporated the need for separate representation and, since November 1976, it has been possible to appoint a guardian ad litem in unopposed revocation of care proceedings—which was seen as a priority at that time and which would have covered Maria Colwell's case.

Full implementation of the legislation, however, had to wait for nine years until May 27th 1984 when it became possible to appoint guardians ad litem in adoption, freeing for adoption and in a range of care and related proceedings, including requests by the local authority to terminate access to a child in care. In addition, the role of reporting officer was introduced specifically to witness the agreement to adoption and to see that it was freely given, informed and unconditional.

In practice guardians ad litem are expected to give paramount consideration to the need to safeguard the child's best interests until he or she achieves adulthood, taking into account the child's wishes and feelings, having regard to his or her age and understanding and ensuring that those wishes and feelings are made known to the court. In carrying out their task, panel members act as independent professionals who provide a non-partisan view to the court. The guardian ad litem therefore acts as a safeguard in a variety of court proceedings in which critical and difficult decisions are being made about children's lives.

Under the Children Act 1989 the role of guardians ad litem is considerably expanded and enhanced. They are to be appointed more often in a wider range of proceedings and, in addition, take on a significant new case management role as set out in section 41 of the Act and the Court Rules. Guardians will be advising courts on allocation and timetabling of cases and will be expected to assist courts in keeping delays to a minimum. In future the timescale should be that of the child, not the adults, and it will be up to guardians ad litem to provide early warning to the courts to prevent harmful delay.

The Children Act 1989 represents a fundamental reform of the law under which children's legislation will be handled through a unified jurisdiction. New court structures offer professionals greater opportunities for a more flexible approach to children's proceedings and the Act requires a different culture in child care law and practice.

The crucial importance of the guardian ad litem's role is that it stands at the interface between the conflicting rights and powers of courts, local authorities, and natural and substitute parents in relation to the child. The guardian has to safeguard the child's interests, to ensure the most positive outcome possible for the child. The guardian also has to make a judgement between the potentially conflicting demands of children's rights, children's rescue, the autonomy of the family and the duty of the state.

Children now move centre-stage and guardians ad litem move with them, to occupy a pivotal role in the successful implementation of the Act.

Chapter 2

Principles and Key Messages of the Act

The Children Act 1989 introduces a number of guiding principles. These are:

- the welfare of the child is the paramount consideration

- wherever possible, children should be brought up and cared for within their own families

- parents with children in need should be helped to bring up their children themselves

- this help should be provided as a service to the child and his family and should:
  * be provided in partnership with the parents
  * meet each child's identified needs
  * be appropriate to the child's race, culture, religion and language
  * be open to effective independent representations and complaints procedures
  * draw upon effective partnership between the local authority and other agencies including voluntary agencies

- children should be safe and be protected by effective intervention if they are in danger

- when dealing with children, courts should ensure that delay is avoided, and may only make an order if to do so is better than making no order at all

- children should be kept informed about what happens to them, and should participate when decisions are made about their future

- parents will continue to have parental responsibility for their children, even when their children are no longer living with them. They should be kept informed and participate when decisions are made about their children's future

A UNIFIED JURISDICTION

The Children Act creates a concurrent jurisdiction for a wide range of family proceedings in new Magistrates' Family Proceedings Courts, County Courts and the High Courts. It is expected that the majority of cases will start in the Family Proceedings Court, but from there they may be directed upwards to the County or High Court, or sideways to other Family Proceedings Courts in different areas. Local authorities' use of wardship is severely restricted and guardians ad litem therefore will have to become more used to the County and High Court venues than has previously been the case.

The reasons for a unified jurisdiction are:

- to simplify and amalgamate complex public and private law, recognising that children may be involved with both;

— to enable all aspects of the case to be dealt with by the same court at the same time (e.g. simultaneous applications for adoption and contact orders in respect of the same child);

— to cut down unnecessary delay in allocating cases to different courts and to expedite hearings by allowing for sideways, as well as upwards and downwards transfer of cases.

THE WELFARE CHECKLIST

For the first time the Act introduces a welfare checklist in section 1(3) which applies to public law cases under Part IV of the Act and contested private law cases and which, under the Court Rules, the court and the guardian ad litem have a duty to consider.

In considering whether or not to make an order, the court shall have regard to:

> *"(a)   the ascertainable wishes and feelings of the child (considered in the light of his age and understanding);*
>
> *(b)   his physical, emotional and educational needs;*
>
> *(c)   the likely effect on the child of any change in his circumstances;*
>
> *(d)   the age, sex and background of the child and any other characteristics of his which the court considers relevant* (this includes the child's race, ethnic origin, culture and religion);
>
> *(e)   any harm which he has suffered or is at risk of suffering;*
>
> *(f)   how capable each of his parents, or any other person in relation to whom the court considers the question to be relevant, is of meeting his needs;*
>
> *(g)   the range of powers available to the court under this Act in the proceedings in question."*

The above list (a)–(f) and the principle of avoidance of delay in section 1(2) are also stated in the Court Rules as duties falling to the guardian.

Guardians will find it helpful to look at the welfare check list alongside the 'Summarised List of 42 Principles' in the Department of Health publication "The Care of Children—Principles and Practice in Regulations and Guidance" (Reproduced in this Manual as Appendix 3).

SOME KEY MESSAGES FROM THE ACT

Points of particular relevance to guardians ad litem:

One Route into Care

The Act establishes one route into care through one set of criteria. Section 31 includes not only the harm that the child is suffering, but also any significant harm that the child is likely to suffer in the future. Looking to the future will allow care proceedings to cover many situations which would formerly have been heard in wardship proceedings in the High Court. The initial criteria to be satisfied before the court will make a care or supervision order are:

> *"(a) that the child concerned is suffering, or is likely to suffer significant harm; and*
>
> *(b) that the harm, or likelihood of harm, is attributable to:*
>
> *(i) the care given to the child, or likely to be given to him if the order were not made, not being what it would be reasonable to expect a parent to give to him; or*
>
> *(ii) the child's being beyond parental control;"*

and section 1(5) the minimum intervention principle

> *"where a court is considering whether or not to make one or more orders under this Act with respect to a child, it shall not make the order or any of the orders unless it considers that doing so would be better for the child than making no order at all."*

'Care' is not defined in the Act, and guardians should therefore be prepared to define the meaning of 'care' for a particular child.

Supervision Orders

Supervision orders can only be granted if the same conditions as are required for care orders are satisfied. The court will use its discretion as to when to make a supervision, rather than a care order. A supervision order can initially be made for a maximum period of one year, although it may be extended to a maximum of three years. It does not give the local authority parental responsibility. Supervision orders may include requirements of a responsible person—that is, a person with parental responsibility for the child, or any other person with whom he is living. These requirements will contribute to the effective use of the order by, for example, ensuring that the child lives at a place specified in directions given by the supervision order. There is also provision at section 38 for the making of an interim supervision order.

New Orders

The Act introduces several new orders, and new procedures for the emergency protection of children. These are aimed at providing a more flexible and creative approach to meeting the needs of individual children:

Section 8 orders

There are four section 8 orders dealing with residence, contact, prohibited steps and specific issues. These are all orders which allow a court in private law proceedings (divorce, adoption etc.) to make arrangements with respect to a child's upbringing. Subject to a number of restrictions, they are also available in public law proceedings. However, a local authority cannot apply for a contact or residence order or have either order made in its favour. A child in care may apply for a residence order but not other section 8 orders.

Residence Order

The residence order settles the arrangements regarding with whom a child is to live. It is the only section 8 order which may be made when the child is in the care of a local authority. It has the effect of discharging a care order;

Contact Order

The contact order replaces the access order under the old law but the two orders are not identical. A contact order requires the person with whom the child is living to allow the child to visit or stay with named persons or to have contact with them. (A section 8 contact order should not be confused with the assumption of reasonable contact and care contact orders under section 34). Contact is a broader concept than access in that it allows also for indirect contact—telephone calls, birthday cards and letters.

Prohibited Steps Order

The prohibited steps order restrains the actions of another person in relation to the child. The only steps that can be prohibited are those that could be taken by parents in meeting their parental responsibility, e.g. seeking to prevent a child being taken out of the country. The order does not impose an absolute prohibition. The steps specified may still be taken with the leave of the court.

Specific Issue Order

The specific issue order enables a parent (and others) to bring a particular question relating to the exercise of parental responsibility to be determined by the court, e.g. a question concerning a child's schooling or health.

Family Assistance Order (Section 16)

This order is designed to offer short term help to a family in conflict or involved in divorce. It is a voluntary order which offers advice, assistance and befriending to families.

Emergency Protection Order (Section 44)

The emergency protection order replaces the old place of safety order and introduces new procedures for the emergency protection of children. It is a short-term order which enables a child to be made safe when he might otherwise suffer harm. Anyone may apply for an emergency protection order, but an order may only be made in the following circumstances:

The court is satisfied that:

(a) *there is reasonable cause to believe that the child is likely to suffer significant harm if*

(i) *he is not removed to accommodation provided by or on behalf of the applicant; or*

(ii) *he does not remain in the place in which he is then being accommodated;"*

(b) *in the case of an application made by a local authority—*

(i) *enquiries are being made with respect to the child under section 47(1)(b); and*

> *(ii)* *those enquiries are being frustrated by access to the child being unreasonably refused to a person authorised to seek access and that the applicant has reasonable cause to believe that access to the child is required as a matter of urgency; or*
>
> *(c)* *in the case of an application made by an authorised person—*
>
> > *(i)* *the applicant has reasonable cause to suspect that a child is suffering, or is likely to suffer, significant harm;*
> >
> > *(ii)* *the applicant is making enquiries with respect to the child's welfare; and*
> >
> > *(iii)* *those enquiries are being frustrated by access to the child being unreasonably refused to a person authorised to seek access and the applicant has reasonable cause to believe that access to the child is required as a matter of urgency." (section 44(1)*

"Significant harm" in this context has the same meaning as in applications for care and supervision orders; it includes ill-treatment as well as impairment of health and development.

The order:

— lasts for eight days with one possible extension of seven days, making a maximum duration of fifteen days;

— may only be extended once;

— may be sought either to remove or detain a child. For example, it would cover a child who is already in hospital but who would be likely to suffer harm if allowed to return home;

— assumes that reasonable contact will be allowed between parents and children;

— allows parents to challenge the order at any time—although the challenge will only be heard after 72 hours—provided they were *not* present at the original hearing;

The application may be heard *ex parte* or on notice.

Child Assessment Order (Section 43)

This is a completely new order which addresses those situations where there is reasonable cause to suspect that a child is suffering significant harm but is not at immediate risk, and the applicant believes that an assessment (medical, psychiatric or other) is required. If the parents are unwilling to co-operate the local authority can apply for a child assessment order.

The order:

— lasts for a maximum of seven days;

— directs the type and nature of the assessment which is to be carried out, and whether the child should be kept away from home for the purposes of the assessment.

The application is to be heard in court with all parties represented.

Education Supervision Order (Section 36)

Non-school attendance is no longer a ground for care proceedings. The education supervision order, which is applied for by the local education authority rather than the social services department, places a child of compulsory school age who is not being properly educated under the supervision of the local education authority. If a care order is made subsequently, the education supervision order automatically ceases.

Wardship

The introduction of "likely harm" as grounds for care proceedings and the package of section 8 orders mean that the need for cases to be heard in wardship is substantially reduced. The local authority is no longer allowed to invoke the inherent jurisdiction of the High Court as an alternative to public care proceedings, except where set out in section 100(4).

The Act renders wardship and care incompatible. Under section 91(4) if a ward of court is committed to care, the wardship ceases to have effect, while under section 100(2) a child in care cannot be made a ward of court.

From October 14th 1991 wards of court in local authority care became section 31 care cases under the transitional arrangements in Schedule 14 of the Children Act 1989 and the children ceased to be wards of court (see also the Commencement and Transitional Provisions Order 1991 (SI 828) and the Commencement No. 2—Amendments and Transitional Provisions Order 1991 SI 1990). At that stage wards could make applications under any of the range of orders open to them under the Children Act 1989 and might wish, for example, to apply to revoke their section 31 care order or apply for residence or contact orders. Children who have been "de-warded" by the implementation of the Act will need to be made aware of the range of possible orders now open to them under the new legislation. Any ward becoming the subject of a care order or otherwise accommodated by a local authority under voluntary arrangements will also be covered by the Review of Childrens Cases Regulations 1991. The regulations place a duty on local authorities, among other things, to inform children of their rights to make applications for the discharge or variation of orders.

Listening to Children

The Act emphasises the need to listen to children and involve them in decision-making, where they have sufficient understanding.

Preventing Family Breakdown

The Act places responsibility on the local authority to prevent family breakdown through the provision of services under Part 3 of the Act, which deals with local authority support services for children and families.

Race and Culture

For the first time, the Act explicitly directs the local authority to give due consideration to the child's religious persuasion, racial origin and cultural and linguistic background in determining matters of welfare (section 22(5)(c)).

Accommodating Children near the Family Home

The Act incorporates much of the Code of Practice on Access by directing local authorities providing accommodation for children to ensure that the accommodation is near the child's home but adds that, where the authority is providing accommodation for siblings, they should be accommodated together (section 23(7) (b)).

Contact

The Act emphasises the importance of contact between parent and child, siblings and the extended family, even and perhaps particularly during the initial period of removal of the child following emergency procedures. There is a new wider concept of access which will include indirect contacts, telephone calls and letters. The assumption of reasonable contact is implicit in all proceedings under the Act.

Introduction of Representation and Complaints Procedures

The Act reflects the move towards more consumer-led services by requiring each local authority to establish representations, including complaints procedures (section 26). The regulations for the procedures are contained in the Children and Young Persons Representations Procedures (Children) Regulations 1991, Statutory Instrument No. 894; and these are set out in Children Act Guidance and Regulations Volume 3—Family Placements and Volume 4—Residential Care. The new procedures reflect a change of ethos also found in the NHS and Community Care Act 1990. The aim is to emphasise the accountability of service providers to service users in all health and social service provision.

Children's Rights to Make Applications on their own Account

In one of the most significant changes, and one with far reaching implications, the Act gives children the right to apply directly to the court for any one of the new range of orders available. Guardians should give information to children about their rights under the Act, and their ability to initiate proceedings on their own behalf.

These major changes brought in by the Children Act 1989 signal not just a change in the law and a consolidation of the former 'patchwork' provision, but also constitute the framework of a new service for children and families.

Chapter 3

The New Court and Administrative Arrangements

THE COURTS

Concurrent Jurisdiction

The courts with jurisdiction to hear proceedings under the Children Act 1989 are the Magistrates' Family Proceedings Court, the County Court and the High Court Family Division. The allocation of cases is governed by the Children (Allocation of Proceedings) Order 1991.

Magistrates' Family Proceedings Courts

Cases involving the local authority will generally start here. Magistrates will hear applications for care and supervision orders, emergency protection orders, child assessment orders, applications for adoption, freeing for adoption, maintenance and domestic violence. In certain specified circumstances cases may be transferred up to the county court. Orders can also be made by this court under other family legislation. Appeals under the Children Act from this court will go to the Family Division of the High Court.

County Courts

There are now four tiers of county court. The 96 non-divorce county courts have no family jurisdiction except for domestic violence injunctions; the 72 divorce county courts can issue all private law family proceedings but matters which are contested will transfer for trial to one of the 102 family hearing centres. 51 of the family hearing centres are also designated as "care centres" and have full jurisdiction in public law matters transferred up from the magistrates' courts. Each care centre has a designated family judge who is specially selected and trained in public law work.

Appeals from the County Court under the Children Act go to the Civil Division of the Court of Appeal and then on to the House of Lords which is the final appeal court on matters of law.

High Court Family Division

The High Court has full jurisdiction to hear all cases regarding children, including private wardship proceedings and appeals under the Children Act from the Magistrates' Family Proceedings Court. Appeals will go to the Civil Division of the Court of Appeal and then to the House of Lords on a matter of law.

Administrative and Monitoring Arrangements

Family Court Services Committees.

A network of family court services committees has been developed around each care centre. Their main purpose is to provide a forum for professional concerns and to discuss legal and welfare issues arising from the principles of the Act. Also to be discussed is the conduct of the various agencies and professions in safeguarding the welfare of children; for example, interviewing techniques and methods of assessment. Each committee is chaired by the designated family Judge and membership will include representatives of the judiciary, barristers, solicitors, the medical profession, police, the probation service, guardians ad litem, social workers, health authorities, magistrates and justices clerks. The local court's administrator acts as committee secretary and provides the link with the family court business committee.

These committees are likely to meet once or twice a year in a conference seminar forum and cover the same catchment area as the Family Court Business Committee.

Family Court Business Committees

Family court business committees have been set up primarily to monitor management of the workload and to make sure that court business is speedily despatched. These committees are concerned with the management of cases in terms of the availability of resources, priorities in relation to other litigation and allocation procedures between courts. The family court business committees acts as the centre of regional liaison, and will concentrate initially on public family law cases. Each one is chaired by the designated Judge, with the court's administrator acting as Secretary. Other members include a district Judge, a justices' clerk, the panel manager from each Guardian ad Litem Panel in the region and representatives of local authority social services and legal departments and the Legal Aid Board.

See Guidance and Regulations Volume 7 Annex J.

These committees relay key messages to the Children Act Advisory Committee chaired by Mrs Justice Booth and whose terms of reference are to advise Ministers and the President of the Family Division on the effective working of the Act.

The efficiency of services under the Children Act generally will depend upon the effectiveness of regional and local liaison. Guardians ad litem should ensure that they are effectively represented at all relevant committees and meetings as they will be an invaluable source of information and feedback, particularly during the early days of implementation.

ORDERS AND APPLICATIONS

For details of the orders and applications guardians should refer to the Children Act 1989 Guidance and Regulations Volume I—Court Orders.

Summary of orders available under the Children Act 1989

Care order—Section 31

Interim care order—Section 31

Supervision order—Section 31

Interim supervision order—Section 31

Care contact order—Section 34

Child assessment order—Section 43

Emergency protection order—Section 44

Recovery order—Section 50

Family assistance order—Section 16

Education supervision order—Section 36

Section 8 Orders

— Residence order

— Contact order

— Prohibited steps order

— Specific issue order

Removal of Alleged Abuser

Although the Act contains no "ouster order" as such, it is suggested that the local authorities should explore the possibility of providing services to, and/or accommodation for, the alleged abuser as an alternative to removing the child from home. This could be on a voluntary basis backed up by the provisions of schedule 2 paragraph 5, which give authorities the discretion to provide assistance with finding alternative housing or cash assistance to the person who leaves the family home.

As an alternative, the non-abusing parent may wish to apply to the County Court for a short term ouster injunction under section 1 of the Domestic Violence and Matrimonial Proceedings Act 1976 or to the Magistrates' Court for an exclusion order under section 16 of the Domestic Proceedings and Magistrates Court Act 1978 (if the couple are married), forcing the alleged abuser out of the home. In addition, where a child has been placed temporarily with foster parents and there is a risk of problems arising from attempted contact by abusing parents, then this may be grounds for the local authority seeking to invoke the inherent jurisdiction of the High Court to protect the child, for example, by granting an injunction keeping parents from going within a specified distance of the child's foster home or school (section 100(3)). Guardians ad litem may wish to consider these alternatives, particularly when looking at parental applications to discharge emergency protection orders and in the preparation of their reports. (See case study—Appendix 4).

COURT STRUCTURE FOR PROCEEDINGS UNDER THE CHILDREN ACT 1989.

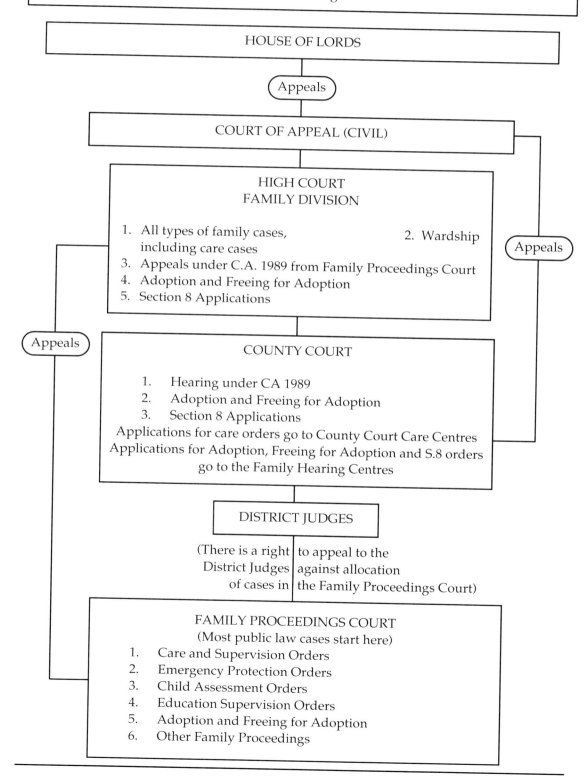

EUROPEAN COURT OF HUMAN RIGHTS
Application may be made in cases of breach of the European Convention on Human Rights

HOUSE OF LORDS

Appeals

COURT OF APPEAL (CIVIL)

Appeals

HIGH COURT
FAMILY DIVISION

1. All types of family cases, including care cases
2. Wardship
3. Appeals under C.A. 1989 from Family Proceedings Court
4. Adoption and Freeing for Adoption
5. Section 8 Applications

Appeals

COUNTY COURT

1. Hearing under CA 1989
2. Adoption and Freeing for Adoption
3. Section 8 Applications

Applications for care orders go to County Court Care Centres
Applications for Adoption, Freeing for Adoption and S.8 orders go to the Family Hearing Centres

DISTRICT JUDGES

(There is a right to appeal to the District Judges against allocation of cases in the Family Proceedings Court)

FAMILY PROCEEDINGS COURT
(Most public law cases start here)
1. Care and Supervision Orders
2. Emergency Protection Orders
3. Child Assessment Orders
4. Education Supervision Orders
5. Adoption and Freeing for Adoption
6. Other Family Proceedings

Chapter 4

The Guardian ad Litem and the Children Act 1989

APPOINTMENT

Section 41 of the Children Act 1989 and the Rules of Court deal with the appointment of guardians ad litem and their duties under the Children Act 1989. Rules for the High Court and County Courts have been harmonised with the rules for the Magistrates' Family Proceedings Courts. The Rules provide for identical functions or tasks, subject to reflecting any structural difference between the Magistrates' Courts on the one hand and the County Court and the High Court on the other. The common core in both sets of Rules is given the same numbering, for ease of reference. In the County Court Rules the provisions in respect of guardians ad litem are in Part IV, and in the Magistrates' Family Proceedings Court Rules in Part II (Rules 10 and 11).

The Act enhances the role of the guardian ad litem in public law proceedings. The requirement to appoint a guardian has been strengthened by extending it to a wider range of proceedings. Guardians will also be appointed earlier in the proceedings so that they can play a full and active role, not only as a representative and spokesperson for the child, but advising the court on matters such as timetabling and directions. No court should adjourn without making a return date for hearing the application. A hearing date, once fixed, cannot be altered except by application to the court. In general, courts will be much more interventionist and will be very firmly in control of all aspects of the conduct of the case, particularly timetabling.

The primary duty of the guardian ad litem is to safeguard the interests of the child. Section 41(1) of the Children Act 1989 directs that *"for the purpose of any specified proceedings the court shall appoint a guardian ad litem for the child concerned unless satisfied that it is not necessary to do so in order to safeguard his interests"*. This is a stronger incentive to the courts to appoint guardians than was the case in the previous provisions and in practice is likely to mean that a guardian is appointed in every public law case, unless there are very strong reasons for not so doing.

A guardian ad litem will be appointed as soon as possible after the commencement of specified proceedings or the transfer of such proceedings to the court unless:

> *"(a)   such an appointment has already been made by the court which made the transfer and is subsisting; or*
>
> *(b)   the justices' clerk or the court considers that such an appointment is not necessary to safeguard the interests of the child." (Rule 10(1))*

Powers of the Parties to the Proceedings to Request the Appointment of a Guardian ad Litem (Rule 10(2) and (3))

At any stage in specified proceedings a party may apply, without notice to the other parties unless the Justices' Clerk or the court otherwise directs, for the appointment of a guardian ad litem (Rule 10(2)). The court will grant such an application unless it considers the appointment not to be necessary to safeguard the interests of the child, in which case it shall give its reasons and a note of such reasons shall be taken by the Justices' Clerk.

Court's Ability to Appoint a Guardian ad Litem (Rule 10(4), (5) (and (6))

At any stage in specified proceedings the Justices' Clerk or the court may, of its own motion, appoint a guardian ad litem. The Justices' Clerk shall then notify other parties and any welfare officer of the appointment of the guardian or, as the case may be, the decision not to make such an appointment (Rule 10(5)). The Justices' Clerk shall send the guardian, as soon as possible after appointment, a Notification of Appointment and serve on the guardian copies of the application and all the documents filed under Rule 17(1). The appointment of a guardian shall continue for such time as is specified in the appointment or until terminated by the court.

Appointment of the Same Guardian ad Litem in Subsequent Proceedings (Rule 10(8))

When appointing a guardian ad litem, the Justices' Clerk or the court shall consider the appointment of anyone who has previously acted as guardian ad litem of the same child. This rule indicates that the court would prefer to appoint the same guardian ad litem who may have acted in applications to discharge emergency protection orders to prepare the report for the final hearing, although in practical terms this may not always be possible.

Termination of Appointment (Rule 10(9) and (10))

The appointment of a guardian ad litem under this Rule shall continue for such time as is specified in the appointment, or until terminated by the court (Rule 10(9)). When the appointment has been terminated the court shall give its reasons in writing and those reasons will be noted by the Justices' Clerk.

Appointment and Non-Appointment of a Guardian (Rule 10(11))

Where the Justices' Clerk or the court appoint or refuses to appoint a guardian, the Justices' Clerk shall record the appointment or the refusal on the appropriate form in schedule 1 to the Court Rules. The Justices' Clerk shall, as soon as practicable, notify the parties and any welfare officer of an appointment under this Rule or, as the case may be, of a decision not to make such an appointment (Rule 10(5)).

Eligibility for Appointment to a Specific Case (Rule 10(7))

A guardian ad litem appointed from a panel shall not:

> *"(a)   be a member, officer or servant of a local authority which, or an authorised person (within the meaning of section 31(9)) who, is a party to the proceedings, unless he is employed by such an authority solely as a member of a panel of guardians ad litem and reporting officers;*
>
> *(b)   be, or have been, a member, officer or servant of a local authority or voluntary organisation (within the meaning of section 105(1)) who has been directly concerned in that capacity in arrangements relating to the care, accommodation or welfare of the child during the five years prior to the commencement of the proceedings;*
>
> *(c)   be a serving probation officer (except that a probation officer who has not in that capacity been previously concerned with the child or his family and who is employed part time may, when not engaged in his duties as a probation officer, act as a guardian ad litem)".*

Guardians should also refer to Chapter 10 of this Manual and the Children Act 1989 Guidance and Regulations Volume 7, Chapter 2.

Volume 7 outlines other situations where it would be prudent for a panel member to seek an alternative appointment. For example, where the panel member has professional or personal links with a person who is or who has been closely involved with the child or family other than as a guardian. This would include the spouse of a panel member who may be employed by the local authority which is party to the proceedings, and who may have direct knowledge of the child or family concerned.

The guidance requires Panels to give a high priority to the need to avoid conflict of interest and a subsequent undermining of independence. Single authority panels are required to ensure that the flexibility to provide suitably independent guardians is not restricted by drawing a large proportion of their membership from the category of employee of the local authority.

The Official Solicitor

Volume 7 discusses the position of the Official Solicitor:

Firstly—under directions arising from the provisions of section 41(8) of the Children Act 1989, the role of the Official Solicitor includes the duty to act as guardian ad litem in High Court proceedings. The proceedings where the Official Solicitor will be appointed are those which commence and are completed in the High Court, or which are allocated to the High Court and where no guardian ad litem has been appointed. If a case is transferred from another level of court to the High Court where a guardian ad litem has been appointed, the Rules of Court allow that the guardian ad litem's appointment may be terminated and a new guardian, ie the Official Solicitor, appointed although this is likely to be the exception rather than the rule. When acting as a guardian ad litem, the Official Solicitor's duties will be those required of all guardians ad litem as set out in Rule 11 of the Rules of Court. The Official Solicitor will not be a member of any Panel of guardians ad litem.

Secondly—Based on their considerable experience and knowledge of High Court procedures and child care cases where wider issues of public policy and complexity are typically present, the Official Solicitor and his staff may act as a reservoir of specialist knowledge and advice to guardians ad litem andreporting officers.

Additionally, the Official Solicitor may be appointed as "amicus curiae" (friend of the court).

PROCEEDINGS IN WHICH GUARDIANS AD LITEM AND REPORTING OFFICERS MAY BE APPOINTED

The range of proceedings in which guardians may be appointed is considerably extended under the Children Act 1989 (see diagram of the Proceedings in which a guardian ad litem and reporting officer may be appointed at the end of this Chapter. Section 41(6) sets out the types of proceedings. These are:

Part IV of the Act—Care and Supervision

- an application for care order or supervision order (section 31);

- arising from family proceedings where the court has directed the local authority to undertake an investigation of the child's circumstances and has made, or is considering whether to make, an interim care order (section 37(1) and 38(1)(a));

- on an application for the discharge of a care order or the variation or discharge of a supervision order under section 39;

- an application to substitute a supervision order for a care order (section 39(4));

- in which the court is considering whether to make a residence order with respect to a child who is the subject of a care order (section 8);

- with respect to contact between a child who is the subject of a care order and any other person (section 34);

- appeals arising from the making, or the refusal to make, a care order, supervision order, contact order or residence order (with respect to a child who is the subject of a care order);

- appeals arising from the variation or discharge (or refusal of an application to vary or discharge) the orders listed in the above paragraph;

- appeals arising from the refusal to substitute a supervision order for a care order.

Part V of the Act—Emergency Protection

- applications for an emergency protection order (section 44);

- applications for a child assessment order (section 43);

- applications for the extension of an emergency protection order (section 45);

- variation and discharge of an emergency protection order (section 43);

- variation and discharge of a child assessment order (section 43);

- appeals arising from the making, or refusal to make, an order under Part V.

Proceedings Specified under Section 41(6)(i)

Under the provisions of this section four additional categories of cases are named as "specified" proceedings in the Family Proceedings Rules and Rule 2 of the Family Proceeding Courts (Children Act 1989) Rules. These are:

— proceedings under section 25 in a family proceedings court for a secure accommodation order;

— applications under section 33(7) for the leave of court to the proposed change of surname for a child who is the subject of a care order or the proposed removal of such a child from the United Kingdom;

— applications under paragraph 19(1) of Schedule 2 for the arranging or assistance in arranging for a child in the care of the local authority to live outside England and Wales;

— applications under paragraph 6(3) of Schedule 3 for the extension or further extension of a supervision order originally made under section 31.

— appeals arising from these proceedings.

Adoption and Freeing for Adoption Proceedings

Guardians ad litem and reporting officers will continue to be appointed in Adoption Proceedings and Freeing Proceedings as set out in the Rules made under section 65 of the Adoption Act 1976.

CASE MANAGEMENT ROLE UNDER THE COURT RULES

Rules of Court give guardians ad litem a substantial new case management role, in particular in assisting the court with the timetabling of cases and the avoidance of delay. Guardians will have a greatly increased scope to investigate the opportunities provided by the creative new private law menu of section 8 orders and to divert proceedings away from Parts IV and V of the Act to the possibility of the provision of services under Part III. This will require a degree of lateral thinking hitherto not required of the service and constitutes one of the most positive and progressive aspects of the new legislation. It will be possible to recommend, for example, a section 8 residence order with a prohibited steps order, or a contact order which would allow an interested member of the extended family to see the child and develop a relationship on a regular basis, whilst specifically prohibiting contact and protecting the child from an alleged abuser. However, it is also expected that courts will be very much more specific about issues to be investigated by guardians.

Representations and Complaints Procedures (Section 26)

Guardians may play an indirect role under the provisions of section 26, which requires local authorities to set up a representations, including complaints, procedure for children in their care and to publicise the arrangements for such procedures.

Section 26(3) lists those people who may make such representations and includes *"such other person as the authority consider has a sufficient interest in the child's welfare to warrant his representations being considered by them"*. This could occasionally include guardians in an individual case about which they are concerned.

The guardian in the course of discussion with children may wish to check that they are aware of how to initiate the local complaints procedure and where to obtain skilled advocacy and support to pursue such complaints. The involvement of guardians directly in complaints procedures does not fall within the role of the guardian ad litem as set out in the Court Rules. Unless the court makes a specific direction requiring the guardian to undertake the work, the guardian will be acting in another capacity and therefore, for example, will be unable to claim travelling or other expenses or use the confidential information derived from their appointment as a guardian. They may however have an important role to play in acting as a bridge to enable the child or young person to use the new procedures, which are a key element in quality control.

The Regulations for the procedures are contained in the Children and Young Persons Representations Procedure (Children) Regulations 1991, Statutory Instrument 1991 No. 894 and in Volumes 3 and 4 of the Guidance and Regulations.

DUTIES OF THE GUARDIAN AD LITEM

Duties of the Guardian and those of the Court((Rule 11(1))

In carrying out their duties guardians must regard themselves as under the same obligation as the court to consider the need to reduce delay (section 1(2)) and to have regard to the matters set out in the Welfare Check-list (section 1(3)(a) to (f)). This provision links the responsibilities of the guardian much more closely to those of the court and emphasises the fact that, in their decision making, the courts will be looking to the guardian for assessment and recommendations.

Attendance at Hearings (Rule 11(4))

The guardian ad litem *must* attend all directions appointments and hearings for the proceedings unless specifically excused by the Justices' Clerk or the court, and shall advise the Justices Clerk or the court on the following matters, which form the basis of the Guardian's case management role :

— whether the child is of sufficient understanding `for any purpose including the child's refusal to submit to a medical or psychiatric examination or other assessment that the court has power to require;

— the wishes of the child in respect of any matter relevant to the proceedings, including the child's attendance at court;

— the appropriate forum for the proceedings, basing the advice on the criteria for transfer of cases:-

   (a) exceptional complexity, importance or gravity;

   (b) the need to consolidate with other proceedings, for example, Adoption and Contact applications;

   (c) urgency;

— the appropriate timetabling of the proceedings, or any part of them always bearing in mind the dictates of section 1(2) regarding the avoidance of delay;

— the options available to it in respect of the child and the suitability of each such option, including what order should be made in determining the application;

— on any other matter on which the Justices' Clerk or the court seeks the guardian's advice or concerning which the guardian considers that the Justices' Clerk or the court should be informed.

Advice to the Court about the Child's Ability to Make an Informed Decision regarding Medical or other Assessment (Rule 11(4) (a))

Under sections 38(6), 43(8) and 44(7) of the Act, and whenever the courts give directions regarding assessment and examination, children have the right to refuse medical, psychiatric or other assessment. Under the Court Rules guardians may advise the court about the ability of the child to make an informed decision regarding their (the child's) consent to medical or other examination. It must be stressed here that it is the role of the guardian to comment on the child's ability to make an informed decision, *not* to persuade the child to undergo such examinations.

However, the question of whether a particular child is of sufficient age and understanding to make a judgement on this matter is peculiarly complex. In the Gillick case—Gillick v West Norfolk and Wisbech Area Health Authority [1986] AC112—it was established that if a child was of sufficient understanding and intelligence to enable it to understand fully what was proposed and to be capable of making up its own mind on the matter, the parental right, and the courts' right, to give or refuse consent yielded to the child's right to make its own decisions whether the child was consenting or refusing consent.

In Re R (a Minor) Wardship: medical treatment as reported in the Times on 31 July 1991, the Master of the Rolls decided in the Court of Appeal that even if a child was "Gillick competent" to refuse consent to treatment, the court could, exercising its wardship jurisdiction, override that refusal if it was in the child's best interest to do so. In summary, the failure or refusal of a child to give consent was very important in the doctor's decision whether or not to treat, but it did not prevent the necessary consent being obtained from another competent source. This case illustrates the complexities inherent in each individual case. Guardians should examine the status of the consent and the competence of the child to give or withhold consent in relation to the age, ability and circumstances of every child and advise the courts accordingly. It is thought that this decision does not override the statutory provisions referred to above concerning the child's refusal to consent to treatment.

Advice to the Court (Rule 11(5))

This may be given either orally or in writing. If the advice is given orally it will be recorded by the Justices' Clerk.

Appointing a Solicitor (Rule 11(2))

The guardian ad litem shall:

> *"(a)   appoint a solicitor to represent the child, unless a solicitor has already been appointed, and*
>
> *(b)   give such advice to the child as is appropriate having regard to his understanding and, subject to Rule 12(1) (a), instruct the solicitor representing the child on all matters relevant to the interests of the child, including possibilities for appeal, arising in the course of any proceedings."*

Divergence of Opinion between the Guardian and the Child (Rule 11 (3))

"Where it appears to the guardian ad litem that the child—

> *(a)   is instructing his solicitor direct, or*

(b)   intends to, and is capable of, conducting the proceedings on his own behalf, he shall so inform the court through the justices' clerk and thereafter -

(i)   shall perform all of his duties under paragraph 2(a) (appointing a solicitor to represent the child) and such other duties as the justices' clerk or the court may direct,

(ii)   shall take such part in the proceedings as the justices' clerk or the court may direct, and

(iii)   may, with the leave of the justices' clerk or the court, have legal representation in his conduct of those duties. "

Some panels have negotiated arrangements with the administering authority whereby the authority undertake to pay any costs involved. Divergence of opinion is most likely to occur in cases where guardians are involved in applications for secure accommodation orders.

In the case of a divergence of opinion between the guardian ad litem and the child who may be of an age and understanding to instruct the solicitor directly or to conduct the proceedings on his own behalf, the guardian ad litem shall inform the court that the child is separately represented. The guardian shall then continue to participate in the proceedings as the court directs. A new provision is that the guardian may have legal representation to help her carry out her duties in relation to the child. In the past, in the case of a divergence of opinion, guardians ad litem have been left without legal representation. Guardians will be able to appoint a solicitor on their own behalf provided they have the leave of the court to do so (Rule 11(3)). The reasonable expenses of such appointments will fall to local authorities to meet.

Termination of the Appointment of a Solicitor (Rule 12(4))

The Court Rules allow the guardian to apply to the court for an order terminating the appointment of the solicitor appointed by the court. However, the solicitor and the child, if he is of sufficient understanding, will be given the opportunity to make representations to the court about such termination of appointment. This provision considerably strengthens the power of the guardians in relation to solicitors representing children and sanctions the ability of the guardian to question the way in which solicitors are carrying out their duties.

Choice of Solicitor

The Law Society publishes lists of solicitors who have been approved as members of their local Children's Panels. ` This list should be available to guardians through their panel manager or local court clerks. Guardians should bear in mind the requirements of each case in making their choice of solicitor. For example, if the case involves allegations of sexual abuse a solicitor with experience of dealing with such cases should be instructed if at all possible. Travelling distances between the solicitor, child, guardian and the court and the need to provide experience for less experienced solicitors on the panel should also be considered. The prime consideration for guardians, however, must be to obtain the best possible representation for a particular child, taking into account that child's particular needs. Care proceedings are still adversarially based and it may be that some cases will require a powerful advocate on behalf of the child, whereas others may require a sensitive one who is able to establish a rapport and communicate with the child directly. In all cases solicitors should see the children they represent, however young, as this will give them a clear picture of their client and his stage of development, thus facilitating the presentation of the child's case in court. It is the child after all who is the solicitor's client, not the guardian ad litem.

Guardians may appoint solicitors who are not members of the Children's Panel, provided they are satisfied that their particular skills meet the requirements of the child's case.

Additional Parties to the Proceedings (Rule 11(6))

The guardian ad litem shall where practicable, notify any person whose joinder as a party to those proceedings would be likely in the guardian's opinion, to safeguard the interest of the child, of that person's right to apply to be joined under rule 7 (2) *"and shall inform the Justices' Clerk or the court:—*

> *(a)   of any such notification given,*
>
> *(b)   of anyone whom he attempted to notify under this paragraph but was unable to contact, and*
>
> *(c)   of anybody who he believes may wish to be joined to the proceedings."*

Under this rule guardians have a wide ranging responsibility to check that all those with parental responsibility are aware of the proceedings and their right to become parties. It is the local authority' s responsibility (or other applicant) to serve notice of the proceedings on the relevant people—eg. all those with parental responsibility.

Accepting Documents on Behalf of the Child (Rule 11(8))

In the absence of a solicitor acting for the child, the guardian shall serve, and accept service of documents on behalf of the child and where the child has not himself been served with the documents and has sufficient understanding, the guardian shall advise the child of the contents of any documents so served.

The Guardian ad Litem's Investigations (Rule 11(9))

In general, guardians have a duty to make such investigations as may be necessary to carry out their duties and shall in particular:

> *"(a)   contact or seek to interview such persons as he thinks appropriate or as the court directs;*
>
> *(b)   if he inspects records of the kinds referred to in section 42, bring to the attention of the court, through the justices' clerk, and such other persons as the justices' clerk or the court may direct, all such records and documents which may, in his opinion, assist in the major determination of the proceedings, and*
>
> *(c)   obtain such professional assistance as is available to him which he thinks appropriate, or which the justices' clerk or the court directs him to obtain."*

Production of a Written Report (Rule 11(7))

"The guardian ad litem shall, unless the justices' clerk or the court otherwise directs, not less than seven days before the date fixed for the final hearing of the proceedings, file a written report advising on the interests of the child ; and the justices' clerk shall, as soon as practicable, serve a copy of the report on the other parties."

Ability of other Parties to Question the Guardian ad Litem about Oral or Written Evidence (Rule 11(11))

Any other party to the proceedings has the right to question a guardian about any oral or written evidence tendered to the Justices' Clerk or the court.

Attendance of the Child at Hearings (Rule 16(2))

Proceedings shall take place in the absence of any party, including the child, if:

> *"(a)   the court considers it in the interests of the child, having regard to the matters to be discussed or the evidence likely to be given, and*
>
> *(b)   the party is represented by a guardian ad litem or solicitor;*

and when considering the interests of the child under sub-paragraph (a) the court shall give the guardian ad litem, solicitor for the child and, if he is of sufficient understanding, the child, an opportunity to make representations."

The guardian should consider this Rule when deciding with the child's solicitor how to deal with any sensitive information which is likely to form part of the hearing.

Giving Reasons for the Court's Decision (Rule 21(6))

"When making an order or when refusing an application, the court, or one of the Justices constituting the court by which the decision is made, shall state any findings of fact and the reasons for the court's decision."

This is a considerable improvement on the previous situation in which courts often made an extremely brief statement of the decision, leaving parents and other parties in a state of confusion and uncertainty about what had been decided and why.

Withdrawal of Applications (Rule 5(4))

If any of the parties seek to withdraw an application the guardian ad litem must be consulted and have an opportunity to make representations. Requests to withdraw applications may be made orally, in which case the guardian must be present, or in writing, in which case the guardian must be heard before the court considers the request. Seven days notice of hearing of request to withdraw applications must be given to all parties, including the guardian ad litem.

Additional Duties (Rule 11(10))

In addition, the guardian shall provide the court with such other assistance as it may require.

EVIDENCE

Order of Evidence

Evidence will normally be heard in the following order:

— the applicant;

— any party with parental responsibility for the child;

— other respondents;

— the guardian ad litem;

— the child, if he is a party to the proceedings and there is no guardian ad litem.

Expert Examination and Assessment of Children (Rule 18)

(1)   No person may, without leave of the justices' clerk or the court, cause the child to be medically or psychiatrically examined, or otherwise assessed, for the purpose of the preparation of expert evidence for use in the proceedings.

(2)   An application for leave under paragraph (1) shall, unless the justices' clerk or the court otherwise directs, be served on all the parties to the proceedings and on the guardian ad litem.

(3)   Where the leave of the justices' clerk or the court has not been given under paragraph (1), no evidence arising out of an examination or assessment to which that paragraph applies may be adduced without the leave of the court".

Although courts are seeking to reduce the numbers of psychiatric or medical examinations or assessments which children have to undergo in relation to the proceedings, particularly now that so many more parties may have parental responsibility, nevertheless courts are likely to look sympathetically on any professional assistance which the guardian feels it is appropriate to obtain. However, the courts may encourage joint examinations by medical representatives of the parties wherever possible.

Hearsay Evidence (section 41(11))

"Regardless of any enactment or rule of law which would otherwise prevent it from doing so, the court may take account of:

> *(a)   any statement contained in a report made by a guardian ad litem who is appointed under this section for the purpose of the proceedings in question; and*

> *(b)   any evidence given in respect of the matters related to in the report, insofar as the statement or evidence is, in the opinion of the court, relevant to the question which the court is considering".*

This means that guardians may produce records containing hearsay evidence in court.

Children's Evidence

Section 96 relaxes the laws of evidence in favour of children to enable their unsworn testimony to be read by the court, provided:

> (a)   he understands that it is his duty to speak the truth; and

> (b)   he has sufficient understanding to justify his evidence being heard.

Third Party Evidence

Courts will be able to give such weight to hearsay evidence as they think fit under orders made by section 96(3) which makes provision for the admissibility of evidence which would otherwise be inadmissible under any rule of law relating to hearsay. In addition, the Children (Admissibility of Hearsay Evidence) Order 1991 (Statutory Instrument No. 1115) abolished the hearsay rule in all children's proceedings from the 14th October 1991. This provides that *"in civil proceedings before the High Court or county court and in family proceedings in a magistrates' court, evidence given in connection with the upbringing, maintenance or welfare of a child shall be admissible notwithstanding any rule of law relating to hearsay."*

RECORDS

Access to Records

Section 42(1) gives guardians a statutory right of access to, and the right to copy, local authority records and to use them in evidence. A separate right of access to NSPCC records is provided for in an amendment to section 42 contained in paragraph 18 of schedule 16 to the Courts and Legal Services Act 1990. This brings the situation into line with that which already existed for the right of access to adoption agency records.

In addition, access to the records of voluntary organisations and registered childrens homes is provided for in the regulations:

"Each voluntary organisation, where they are not acting as an authorised person, and every person carrying on a registered children's home, shall provide a guardian ad litem of a child—

> *(a)   such access as may be required to—*

>> *(i)   case records and registers maintained in accordance with these Regulations; and*

>> *(ii)   the information from such records or registers held in whatever form (such as by means of computer);*

(b)   such copies of the records and entries as he may require." (Regulation 11, Children and Young Persons Arrangements for Placement of Children (General) Regulations 1991 (Statutory Instrument No. 890))

"Each voluntary organisation, where they are not acting as an authorised person, and every person carrying on a registered children's home shall provide a guardian ad litem of a child-

(a)   such access as may be required to—

(i)   records in so far as they relate to the child maintained in accordance with these Regulations; and

(ii)   the information from such records held in whatever form (such as by means of computer);

(b)   such copies of the records and entries as he may require." (Regulation 16, Children and Young Persons Children's Homes Regulations 1991 (Statutory Instrument No. 1506))

Medical Records

Guardians have no statutory right of access to medical records, except where they form part of the social services file documents.

Appeals

Rule 11(2)(b) requires that the guardian ad litem shall instruct the solicitor representing the child on all matters relevant to the interests of the child including possibilities for appeal, arising in the course of proceedings. Appeals must be lodged within twenty-one days of the originating order. Appeals from Family Proceedings courts go to the High Court Family Division while appeals from the County Court go to the Court of Appeal Civil Division.

Confidentiality of Documents (Rule 23)

"No document, other than a record of an order, held by the court and relating to relevant proceedings shall be disclosed, other than to—

(a) a party

(b) the legal representative of a party

(c) the guardian ad litem

(d) the Legal Aid Board, or

(e) a welfare officer

without leave of the justices' clerk or the court."

PROCEEDINGS IN WHICH A GUARDIAN AD LITEM OR REPORTING OFFICER MAY BE APPOINTED

CASE MANAGEMENT ROLE (S41 (10))

(applies to proceedings under the Children Act 1989)

Includes
- time tabling and allocation of cases
- considering whether the order applied for or any other is appropriate
- accepting service of documents on behalf of the children

CARE AND SUPERVISION (PART IV CHILDREN ACT 1989)

1. Applications FOR and TO DISCHARGE:— CARE ORDERS and SUPERVISION ORDERS (S31)
2. Where the court are considering CONTACT for children in care (S34)
3. Where the court is considering a S.8 RESIDENCE ORDER for children in care.
4. Where a CARE ORDER is being considered in proceedings arising from S37 (1)
5. Substituting a SUPERVISION ORDER for a CARE ORDER (S39 (4))
6. Related APPEALS

ADOPTION AND FREEING FOR ADOPTION (SECTION 65 Adoption Act 1976)

1. ADOPTION
2. FREEING FOR ADOPTION
3. APPOINTMENT OF REPORTING OFFICER

GALROS to be appointed

PROTECTION OF CHILDREN (PART V Children Act 1989)

Applications FOR and:
TO DISCHARGE –
1. EMERGENCY PROTECTION ORDERS (S44)
2. CHILD ASSESSMENT ORDERS (S43)
3. Advice to Court on child's ability to make an informed decision re. medical or other assessment (S43)
4. Related APPEALS

SPECIFIED PROCEEDINGS SECTION 41 (6) (i) (Children Act 1989)

Applications for:
1. SECURE ACCOMMODATION ORDERS (S25)
2. Children in Care to live outside England and Wales (Sch. 2 Para. 19.1)
3. Changing Child's Surname or removing him from the UK while a care order is in force (S 33 (7))
4. extending or further extending a SUPERVISION ORDER (Sch 3. Para 6 (3))
5. Related APPEALS

PART II

THE TASK

Chapter 5

The Task of the Guardian ad Litem in Proceedings under the Children Act 1989

(This chapter may be particularly useful for guardians ad litem undergoing induction training)

PRACTICAL APPROACHES

The role and task of the guardian ad litem and reporting officer in adoption and freeing for adoption proceedings is set out in Part IV of the Manual.

The role of the guardian ad litem is critical in safeguarding the interests of the child. It can involve professional isolation and anxiety but it can bring great rewards, in that panel members are in a unique position to influence events on behalf of the child at a crisis point in a life which will already have involved painful experiences of loss and uncertainty. In order to understand what is best for the future, the Guardian must understand the child's past and the skein of inter-relationships and events which have influenced the child's actions and understanding. Carrying out the investigation is rather like being presented with a large and intricate jigsaw puzzle—all the pieces have to fit together correctly otherwise the picture is blurred and distorted and makes no sense. Each piece of information has to be examined to see where it fits, and this is a complex process requiring patience, clear sight, an open mind, and painstaking attention to detail.

Remember that the guardian's task is a time-limited, task-centred one with a particular end in view—the acquiring of enough knowledge over a short space of time to present the court with a reasoned and coherent view of the child's situation, the options available to the court and a clear recommendation of the course of action which would be in the child's best interests for the future.

The task may broadly be divided into four stages:

Stage One   —Preliminary

Stage Two   —Investigative

Stage Three   —Reporting

Stage Four   —After the hearing

(The reporting stage includes preparing a report and representing the child, both in and out of court).

The following checklists are not prescriptive or exclusive but they are intended to provide indications of the guardian's potential range of tasks. In each case, and depending on the circumstances and the time scale, the guardian will have to exercise her professional judgement and prioritise accordingly. All checklists are aids to the exercise of professional discretion, not a substitute for it.

Stage One—Preliminary

Check list

1. What is the particular expertise required of a guardian in this case? Is the guardian free to act immediately and to keep within a reasonable timetable without incurring unnecessary delay? (section 1(2)).

   Any estimates of time should allow for possible adjournments, court waiting time, the preparation of the report, studying relevant reports and the local authority file and attending any necessary post-hearing conferences. Is the guardian free to act, unhampered by any professional conflict of interest to their independence? For example, if a guardian has previous knowledge of the family involved, that would involve a professional conflict of interest.

2. Identify the nature of the proceedings, the applicants and the local authority involved.

3. Has the guardian received the appropriate application form and order of appointment form from the court? The form should include adequate and accurate details of:—

— the child;

— the nature of, and grounds for, the application;

— whether or not a solicitor has been appointed;

— the child's immediate and extended family;

— all those with parental responsibility;

— current and proposed plans for contact;

— the long term plan for the child, if the order applied for is made.

4. Ensure that the child is a party to the proceedings and that other prospective parties have also been informed of their eligibility to be joined as parties.

5. Check if a solicitor has been appointed. If so, is the guardian happy with the choice? The Court Rules allow the guardian to change the solicitor if this is appropriate.

6. Check the date of the hearing and the court in which it will take place.

7. Identify where the child is living and what is his state of knowledge about the proceedings in question.

8. Identify who, within the local authority, is making the decisions about the child.

9. What are the existing arrangements for reasonable contact (if the child is not residing at home)?

Preliminary Action Plan

1. Scrutinise the application form and all documentation supplied by the court. If the information is inadequate or incomplete refer back to the applicant for full information to be made available without further delay.

2. Appoint a suitable solicitor and ensure that the child has Legal Aid. Under the Legal Aid Regulations the means and merits test in care and certain other related proceedings are waived in favour of parents and children where they are parties.

3. Liaise with the court in connection with the guardian's functions under Rule 11(4), e.g. allocation of the case. Is it appropriate that the case should start in the Magistrates'

Family Proceedings Court, or does its complexity warrant transfer to the County, or even High Court?

4. Check that the local Family Proceedings Court is likely to be able to deal with this case within a reasonable amount of time. If not should a "sideways" transfer be considered to another Family Proceedings Court in a different area? Are the complexities such that vertical transfer would be appropriate? What would the logistics of such a transfer involve in terms of the arrangements to be made in respect of parties and witnesses for the final hearing? (Guardians may wish to review the question of the appropriate venue for the hearing in the light of additional information).

5. Inform the local authority and the social worker responsible for the child of your appointment, both in writing and by telephone.

6. Open a file and begin to compile a record and information sheet including the date of appointment, the addresses, telephone numbers and essential information about relevant parties and professionals involved. Start to fill in a timesheet of time spent on the case.

7. Make a preliminary list of people who will need to be seen.

8. Arrange a first meeting with the child and the child's solicitor.

9. Identify the powers and duties of the guardian appropriate to this particular case.

10. Check that arrangements for reasonable contact under section 34 are working satisfactorily for the child (if the child is away from home).

11. Ensure that parents are being kept informed of the local authority's plans for the child.

12. Seek directions from the court on any particular matter if necessary.

Stage Two—Investigative

It may be helpful to divide this stage into two parts:

1. **Information gathering**—covering the broad range of necessary information.

2. **Targeting the investigation**—on aspects of the case which are either in dispute or which require more detailed investigation.

Information Gathering

As part of the information gathering exercise, the guardian will interview or speak to all those named in the preliminary list. She will also examine the local authority records and, most importantly, work out a coherent plan of work with the child over the period of her involvement. She should tell the child, if he is old enough, when and how often she will be visiting and she should stick to the arrangement. The child should be seen in all aspects of his environment, including with the natural parents, the foster parents and in the school or nursery. The guardian must make a judgement about how wide ranging this aspect of the investigation should be. At this stage the guardian will be focusing on key aspects:

— an analysis of the local authority records. Guardians should establish the dates of and reasons for decisions taken by the local authority;

— consideration of whether or not the order sought, or any other, is appropriate, e.g. are the threshold criteria for the making of an order under section 31 met?

— the contacts the child wishes to have and should be having, at this stage in the proceedings (bearing in mind that the guardian may wish to see the child with his parents as part of the investigation);

— The timetabling of the case, making sure no "slippage" is occurring;

— consultation with the child's solicitors about the conduct of the investigation. One of the purposes of the Directions Appointment is to help identify matters that are in dispute. If the court is exercising proper case management, the guardian can expect a clear steer as to the specific issues that require investigation.

Once the guardian has familiarised herself with all aspects relevant to the case it may well be that the problems, or key issues, will be found to revolve around one particular aspect, person or group of people involved with the case or around an area of disputed evidence. For example, it may be that the key questions are about whether or not the natural mother in the case is able to protect her child from the risk of further abuse, or whether or not the foster carers involved in fact wish to be considered as adoptive parents for the child, or are unhappy about continuing contact. It may be that there have been problems in the management of or communication about the case by the social services department or that other professionals involved, such as the police or the health visitor, have played a very significant role in the history of the proceedings. At this stage, however, the guardian ad litem should be narrowing the focus and *targeting investigations* on the area which will yield the most helpful and additional information. It is possible that there is some relative or member of the extended family who has not been interviewed before, or there may be a person of key importance in the child's life who has not been recognised as such in the past. The activities of the social services department need to be examined and having ascertained the policies and practices of the particular local authority the guardian should relate those policies and practices to the needs of this particular child. Some local authorities adopt blanket policies which may be unsuitable for the child the guardian represents. This can be particularly true in the sensitive area of trans-racial adoption or in relation to children with special needs.

Action plan for information gathering

1. What, in this initial stage, appear to be the key issues in the case? Flowing from this, what records need to be read and who needs to be interviewed?

2. Make written appointments to see all concerned parties and people; the order in which people are seen should be determined by the circumstances of each case. As a general rule the guardian should see the child as soon as possible after appointment unless there are good reasons for not so doing.

3. Carry out initial interviews with all relevant people, not forgetting the extended family, previous foster carers, teachers and residential care staff if any. The key word here is "relevant". Guardians should be clear in their own mind about *why* they are seeing somebody— with a view to obtaining *what* information?

4. *Check up carefully on any member of the household who is an unknown quantity.* There will be local arrangements for checking criminal records;

5. Continue to see the child in order to keep him fully apprised of all relevant information;

6. Gather together and assimilate all relevant written information, previous social enquiry reports, assessments from observation and assessment centres, medical reports etc.

7. List those with parental responsibility. For example, where a mother has divorced and remarried, and where a second husband has been granted a residence order in favour of the children of the first marriage, then there are three people with parental responsibility, all of whom have certain rights in the proceedings and in relation to contact.

8. Re-assess the need for any additional interviews either with those already interviewed or with new people, in the light of new information.

9.   Review the documents already obtained and read. There may be others which are also relevant as the case progresses.

10.   Alert the Panel Manager to any exceptional requirements or circumstances of the case.

Local authority records

Particular care should be taken when the guardian is reading local authority records to separate matters of fact and opinion. She should be particularly careful to identify circumstances in which hearsay evidence has been allowed to acquire the status of truth through frequent repetition e.g. the father is uninterested in his child or the mother is inadequate. Guardians have to become very adept at sifting the information in files e.g. establishing a chronological order of events and the point at which decisions were taken and why. Case conference and review minutes are good building blocks for reconstructing and examining the key elements of the case.

Manner of child's removal

The guardian ad litem should look extremely closely at what happened on the day or night of any child's removal from home. It is often at this point that things can go wrong, *firstly* in that children may run the risk of being traumatised by an abrupt removal, and *secondly* because natural parents can quickly become alienated from the social workers, thus undermining the possibilities of working in partnership in the future. It should be possible under the Children Act 1989 for children to be admitted to accommodation or care as parts of a constructive plan, rather than as a result of a "dawn raid". The guidance given in "Working Together": Paragraph 3.8 says:

> "The removal of children from their home gives rise to public and professional concern, causes great distress if not handled sensitively, and can be damaging both for the child and for the rest of the family. Therefore, except when a child is in acute physical danger it is essential that the timing of the removal of children from their homes should be agreed following consultation with all appropriate professionals. They should weigh up the likely immediate and long term effects of removing the child against the possibility of harm if they leave the child at home, and balance this with the need to secure evidence of criminal offences, and, in some cases, to arrest the suspects. In other cases, however, particularly those involving several children and adults in different households, it may be important to prevent suspects from communicating with each other or destroying evidence. In those cases it may be necessary for co-ordinated police action, distressing though this may be, at a time of day when the whole family is at home. In other cases although early morning police action might secure better forensic evidence, such action may not be crucial to the overall welfare of the child(ren) and should not therefore be part of the plan for investigation. In all cases the long term protection of and well-being of the child will be the overriding concern; the likelihood of securing the child's well being through the courts will be an important consideration."

Guardians should alert the court to any secondary abuse the child may be suffering or have suffered during or after the removal, bearing in mind that it is not part of the social work task to acquire evidence for criminal proceedings, but to ensure that the child receives adequate protection.

Criminal Proceedings—Evidence

Section 98 of the Children Act 1989 is intended to ensure that relevant evidence is brought before the court in care and related proceedings under Parts IV and V of the Act. A statement or admission which may incriminate a person or his or her spouse and which is given in the course of such proceedings cannot be used in evidence against the person making it or his or her spouse in proceedings for an offence other than injury. Accordingly no person is excused from giving evidence of this nature on the basis that it might incriminate themselves or their spouse. (Para 3.17 Working Together).

The guardian should not attempt to appear in court as an expert witness in matters on which she is not competent and credible in the court's eyes as this can only undermine the child's case. The guardian is expected to be an expert in general child care matters, not an expert in specialist areas. On the other hand, the guardian should consider carefully and weigh the benefits against the disadvantages of subjecting the child to excessive medical or psychiatric examination or assessment. There is a general assumption to avoid repeated examination of children already traumatised by primary abuse and removal from home.

Targeting the Investigation—Action Plan

1. *Carry out focused interviews with key people* who may have, or have had, the greatest impact or involvement with the child. Be clear about the purpose of the interviews and what specific information you are hoping to obtain. Some of these interviews may be carried out in conjunction with the solicitor. If it is a question of obtaining witness statements or affidavits it will be appropriate to involve the solicitor in the process.

2. *Working with the child.* It may be that at this stage of the investigation the guardian is particularly involved in work with the child who is, after all, the best person to provide any necessary information. The guardian will want to focus on the child's wishes and see that the child participates in the decision making process, without bearing the responsibility for the decisions made.

3. *Continue to liaise with the court* and keep it informed of all developments. Request a hearing for directions if necessary. Remember that it is appropriate to request a hearing solely on the time tabling of the case.

4. *Discuss your thinking with the local authority* in order to identify possible areas of conflict, agreement, or confusion.

5. *Discuss the conduct of the case* with the child's solicitor.

At the end of the investigation stage, guardians ad litem should:

— be in full possession of the facts relevant to the case;

— have interviewed, or spoken to all those she considers relevant to the proceedings;

— be in a position to represent the child's wishes and feelings to the court;

— be in a position to inform the court on all aspects of the section 1(3) welfare check-list;

— have addressed relevant issues of race, language, culture, religion and disability;

— be in a position to appraise critically the work of the local authority and other agencies in relation to the child;

— be satisfied with the arrangements made for the hearing of the case and the timetable to be followed, i.e. that the case is being heard in the appropriate forum within a reasonable timetable, so that the case will be decided on its facts and not through passage of time;

— be satisfied with the arrangements regarding contact under section 34. In particular are all those involved co-operating with the directions of the Court in this matter? How are the arrangements affecting the child? Do they need variation in the light of experience?

— be in a position to advise the court of the options available to it and the effects on the child of each course of action, including the child's attendance at court;

— put a view to the court regarding section 1(5)—whether making an order will be better than making no order at all;

— be in a position to make a clear recommendation to the court about the course of action to be followed in the best interests of the child;

— be ready to advise the court regarding the conditions to be attached to any order made;

— be clear with the child's solicitor about the evidence to be given by witnesses on behalf of the child;

— inform the local authority of the recommendation she is intending to make.

Recording

Notes of the guardian's interviews should either be recorded contemporaneously or immediately after interview, so they can be used, if needed, as evidence in court.

Timesheets

Fill in timesheets showing clearly the division of time between the various aspects of the case, i.e., interviewing, travelling and attending court.

Stage Three—Reporting and Representing the Child in Court

Since panels of guardians ad litem and reporting officers were introduced, courts have welcomed and have come to reply on GALRO reports. As the Children Act 1989 introduces very substantial changes in the role and powers of the guardian ad litem, so the reports must reflect those changes.

Guardians should take account of the fact that there may be no social enquiry report from the local authority. The local authority's case will usually be contained in the relevant application form and in the witness statements. The guardian's report therefore assumes an enhanced significance as possibly the only comprehensive and free-standing report available to the court.

Presentation of the Evidence

"Decisions can only be as good as the evidence on which they are based and if evidence is distorted, ignored, or not weighed up carefully, the decision will be flawed. They may even be dangerous if risks and benefits are not analyzed and balanced objectively." ("Patterns and Outcomes in Child Placement—Messages from current research and their implications", HMSO 1991). All guardians should read this publication before embarking on presenting their evidence. It is a sequel to "Social Work Decisions in Child Care" (HMSO 1985) and aims to make recent research findings available to social workers in a way which is both easily digestible and informative. Guardians should avoid the "I think, I feel" approach to the presentation of evidence. Perhaps the most important message from recent research is that if progress is to be made in developing professional standards in the care of children, then more attention must be given to accurate descriptions and careful weighing of evidence. Guardians must take care to highlight, throughout their reports, in the light of available knowledge, the facts which have led them to the conclusions. Loose generalisations should be avoided (e.g. "this mother is inadequate and the child is in need of reparenting"). The aim is to present hard evidence not

impressions. Guardians should also be prepared to be challenged on the assumptions and value judgements implicit in their recommendations. In general it is more helpful to the court to describe the behaviour which has led to the judgement made, than to make an assertion palpably open to interpretation. Instead of "this man is a heavy drinker"; "this man drinks on average the equivalent of 50 units of alcohol a week".

Guardians will find the "The Care of Children—Principles and Practice in Regulations and Guidance" (HMSO 1989) a very useful reference point.

REPORTS

Under the Children Act 1989 guardians ad litem are appointed to a very wide-ranging group of proceedings covering a great variety of situations. It follows therefore that their reports cannot all follow the same format, but must aim primarily to make available to the court in as accurate and succinct a manner as possible the necessary information. Where the focus of the enquiry is narrower, the report may be shorter to cover the particular issues under consideration.

Reports should avoid repetition if possible, or duplicating large "chunks" of indigestible facts, which may or may not be strictly relevant. In preparing their reports, guardians should pay strict attention to:

— the requirements of the welfare checklist (Section 1(3)), each aspect of which should be clearly signposted in the report;

— the wishes and feelings of the child, *always* included as a separate section;

— making an unequivocal and logically reasoned recommendation;

— the need to define 'reasonable contact';

— whether making an order will be better than making no order at all (section 1(5)).

Guardians should not wait until the final hearing to bring to the court any serious inacuracies or omissions in the application forms, as this may lead to unnecessary delay. Instead, these should be drawn to the attention of the court and the applicants as soon as they are identified so that the necessary investigations can be made.

Department of Health guidance on Reports to the Courts is being prepared, and will replace previous guidance published by HMSO in 1987.

Format of the Report

This suggested format is suitable for use in proceedings under Part IV of the Act — Care and Supervision Orders. This format is not prescriptive and should be adapted by guardians to meet the requirements of each individual case.

No agency headed paper should be used. The Report should be marked CONFIDENTIAL. Each paragraph should be numbered.

Section 1 — Front page

Name of child/children (if there are siblings then there should be a separate section in respect of each child named in the application)

Case Number (to be used in applications)

Birth date and age of child/children

Type of proceedings (relevant sections and sub-section of the Act)

Court

Statement of Order sought

Date of Hearing

Guardian ad litem report prepared by: Name

Date of appointment

Section 2

(i)   In preparing this report I have interviewed the following people (list of everyone interviewed with dates, number of occasions seen, relationship to the child/children).

(ii) I have spoken to the following on the telephone (name, relationship, date).

(iii) I have attempted to interview the following, but have not done so for the following reasons (if relevant).

(iv) Make a statement of any special matter you wish to bring to the attention of the court. If you have a particular concern about this child, or about any particular aspect of the case, it is helpful to the court to have early warning of this. For example, there may have been a breakdown of communication between the police and the social services department, or some adverse policy or practice which may work to the detriment of other children, or you may be concerned about some practical aspect of the case (for example, timetabling or allocation), which could be notified under this section.

Section 3

Suggested outline

(1)   STATEMENT OF THE ORDER BEING SOUGHT AND BY WHOM, including:

   *   a summary of the nature and outcome of any previous orders or applications, including a consideration of any avoidable delay (section 1 (2));

   *   a statement of any particular matters arising or omitted from the information on the application form;

   *   a statement of any existing directions given either to the court or the guardian.

(2)   CHRONOLOGICAL HISTORY OF THE CASE, including:

   *   the structure of the family, including siblings, the wider extended family and individuals of central importance in the child's life;

   *   statement of the sequence of events which either precipitated or informed the application and the decisions made in relation to the child.

—   This should not be an open-ended section, but should focus on the aspects of the history of direct relevance to the case.

(3)   INFORMATION ABOUT THE CHILD (if not included on the Application form), including:

   *   a list of those who have parental responsibility; (if this is fully listed on the application form it may not be necessary to duplicate)

   *   *section 1(3)(d)*—his age, sex, background and any other relevant characteristics;

   *   —in particular this section should include information about the child's race, culture, religion and list the languages spoken and understood by the child. It should also examine any issues of disability and gender relevant to the case; (none of this information is required on the application form, so guardians should always include it)

   *   *section 1(3)(b)* —a statement of the child's physical, emotional and educational needs, including any special needs or requirements. The guardian should be satisfied that there is full medical information available and that the parents' knowledge of the child's history is recorded. Steps should be taken to ensure that wherever possible there is no disruption to the child's education and that where there has been a change of school full information is transferred.

(4) THE LOCAL AUTHORITY (OR OTHER APPLICANT'S) PLAN FOR THE CHILD, including:

* a critical appraisal of the local authority's policy and practice in relation to this particular child, including any harm the child has suffered or is likely to suffer

* a statement of the proposed arrangements for the child;

* an appraisal of the services provided to the child and his family under Part III of the Act — services to Children and their Families. What positive steps have the local authority taken to keep the family together?

* if the application is for the discharge or variation of a care or supervision order the guardian should consider the requirements on local authorities under the Review of Children's Cases Regulations 1991;

(5) ARRANGEMENTS FOR REASONABLE CONTACT, including:

* a clear statement of who the child is seeing and in what circumstances, with particular reference to contact with siblings;

* how these arrangements are working out in practice;

* any views the other parties or those with parental responsibility may have about the existing or proposed arrangements;

* are they "reasonable"?

(6) THE CAPACITY OF THE CHILD'S PARENTS/CARERS TO MEET THE CHILD'S PRESENT NEEDS (section 1(3)(f)), including:

* an assessment of risk factors;

* section 1(3)(e) — a statement of any harm the child has suffered or is likely to suffer;

* section 1(3)(f) — how capable each of his parents, and any other person in relation to whom the court considers the question to be relevant, is of meeting his needs.

(7) THE WISHES AND FEELINGS OF THE CHILD, including:

* section 1(3)(a) — a clear statement of the child s ascertainable wishes and feelings;

* any written or drawn material prepared by the child (this section should not include the guardian's own views about any of the child's statements).

(8) THE GUARDIAN'S SUMMARY AND ASSESSMENT OF THE CHILD'S SITUATION, including:

* giving a clear picture of the child's present situation;

* highlighting any areas of special need or concern including any disadvantage or discrimination the child may have suffered.

(9) OPTIONS AVAILABLE TO THE COURT

* *section 1(3)(g)* —"the range of powers available to the court under this Act in the proceedings in question", including:

* a clear statement of the options, making full use of the menu of section 8 orders and range of other orders available under the Act with a reasoned analysis of the likely effects of the different courses of action. This should include consideration of the merits of an interim supervision order with a section 8 residence order as a way of avoiding removal from home.

(10) *section 1(5)* —WILL MAKING AN ORDER BE BETTER THAN MAKING NO ORDER AT ALL, including:

* a statement of why the order is or is not justified, e.g. have the threshold criteria been met;

* a statement of whether making an order will be better than making no order at all, even if the conditions for the making of an order have been satisfied. In making this judgement guardians should be aware of the likely outcome for the child, e.g. is there a suitable placement available which will meet the needs of this particular child?

(11) RECOMMENDATION

The guardian's recommendation should:

(a) be clearly stated;

(b) be logically reasoned and related to the evidence;

(c) make full use of the menu or orders available under the Act;

(d) incorporate positive features of the child's life, while attempting to offset the effects of the negative;

(e) consider the powers available to the local authority under Part III of the Act as an alternative to the making of a court order;

(f) allow the child's participation in the decision making, if of appropriate age and understanding;

(g) include the guardian's recommendations for contact. The recommendation should include advice to the court regarding arrangements for contact under section 34(5). It may include short or extended visits involving overnight stays or it may be limited to indirect contact through letters or telephone calls. The guardian must define the purpose of the contact:

in meeting the child's needs; and

in forming part of the plan for this particular child. Contact may be:

(i) part of a plan for reuniting the child with his family;

> (ii) to maintain constructive and consistent links with people who are important in the child's life;
>
> (iii) increasing the child's sense of security and comfort through a particularly difficult time, e.g. while awaiting the outcome of court proceedings.
>
> (h) allow the development of the child's unique identity, taking into account issues of race, culture and religion;
>
> (i) offer minimum disruption;
>
> (j) allow the child hope of a positive future;
>
> (k) include any conditions to be attached to any order made. Section 11(7) provides the power to attach conditions and directions to a section 8 order.

Stage Four—After the hearing

After the hearing there are some matters which the guardian will need to consider:

— does the child understand the outcome of the proceedings and the implications for their future?

— is it appropriate to consider lodging an appeal on behalf of the child?

— are there are matters of policy or practice on which the guardian ad litem wishes to comment formally to the local authority?

— are there matters about the conduct or procedure of the case which the guardian would like to be conveyed to the Panel Manager for discussion at the Family Court Business Committee?

— has the guardian arranged for the confidential and secure storage of one report and return or shredded confidential case material and reports?

— is the child eligible for compensation through the Criminal Injuries Compensation Scheme?

— is the child aware of his right to make applications to the court on his own account, to vary, discharge or apply for orders under the Act? This includes applying for leave to make an application for a section 8 order where appropriate.

— is the child aware of his rights to make representations under section 26 if he is distressed or worried by some aspect of his care, and of his rights to have access to an independent person, and to services of advice and advocacy to assist him in making his representations?

Criminal Injuries Compensation Scheme (Criminal Justice Act 1988)

It is possible that children and young people who have been involved in public care proceedings may be eligible for criminal injuries compensation, particularly those who have been subjected to physical or sexual abuse. Application forms are available from the Criminal Injuries Compensation Board and should be made within three years of the injury taking place. Guardians should advise children on their eligibility for compensation under this scheme.

THE TASK OF GUARDIAN AD LITEM –
Component Parts

INFORMATION GATHERING

Interviewing:—

- The Child/Children
- Parents/Carers/Relative
- Professionals:— Social Workers, G.P., Health Visitor, Paediatrician, Teacher, Nursery Staff, Child Psychologist/Psychiatrist.
- Any other person with an interest in the child.

ASSESSING INFORMATION
Reading and Analysing:-

- Cases files
- Witness Statements & Reports
- Documents relating to the case
- Contracts between parents and SSDs

Evaluating the evidence

- incorporating the Guardian's own observations

MANAGING THE CASE

Liaising with the court re:-

- Avoiding delays S1 (2) — working to a timetable
- Allocation of case to appropriate court
- Receiving documents on behalf of the child if no solicitor has been appointed.
- Ensuring that all those with parental responsibility are aware of:—
    - a) the proceedings
    - b) their right to be represented

REPRESENTING THE CHILD
- Ascertaining the child's wishes and feelings
- Appointing and working with the child's solicitor
- Preparing the case, including expert witness evidence
- Writing a report and making a recommendation.
- Attending all court hearings including *all* directions hearings.

PROFESSIONAL DEVELOPMENTS
- Attending panel business and support group meetings
- Professional consultation
- Training and reading relevant journals
- Participation in regular review & evaluation
- Setting up and administering clerical systems, including the typing of reports and the confidential storage of documents.

Chapter 6

Proceedings in which the Guardian is Appointed

For Adoption and Freeing for Adoption see Part IV of the Manual. See also diagram on page 31

CARE AND SUPERVISION UNDER PART IV OF THE ACT

Care and Supervision Orders

The court hearing an application for care order or supervision order may make any section 8 order as an alternative to a care or supervision order, or in combination with a supervision order either on application or on its own initiative.

Conditions

The child must be under the age of seventeen (or under sixteen if married). The order ceases when the child reaches the age of eighteen and it is no longer possible to extend the period of care to the age of nineteen in certain circumstances.

The significance of the harm should not necessarily be equated with the severity of the injuries. A cigarette burn, for example, can be highly significant as an indication of premeditated harm to the child.

Interim orders

The Act gives the courts new powers to make an interim supervision order as an alternative to an interim care order. An interim supervision order may also be linked to a short term residence order and parents or other parties to the proceedings will have the right to challenge an interim order either by appeal *or* by applying to discharge the order.

There are two reasons for the new powers to make interim orders. *Firstly* to enable the child to be suitably protected while proceedings are progressing and *secondly* to ensure that an order lasts only as long as necessary. Interim care or supervision orders can be made pending a hearing for a full care or supervision order or pending the outcome of a local authority's investigation under section 37(1) arising out of family proceedings.

Criteria

The test is not the same as a full care order. The court must be satisfied (whether the making of an interim order is contested or not), that there are *reasonable grounds* for believing that the child's circumstances fulfil the criteria for a full care or supervision order under section 31. This is a lesser test than a full order which requires proof that the child is suffering or likely to suffer significant harm. It would not be realistic to require such proof at the interim stage as this would pre-empt the outcome of the guardian ad litem's final report and a full investigation of the case.

Guardians therefore should actively consider interim supervision or care orders as an alternative available to the child. They should, however, make it absolutely clear to parents and other parties that their support for making an interim order relates to an interim period and does not pre-judge the final outcome.

Furthermore, the use of an interim supervision order combined with a section 8 residence order could be a very creative option as it would give the guardian and the local authority a chance to assess the likely long term outcome of such an arrangement and the practicality of building such orders into future arrangements. If, for example, a suitable relative or other person connected with the child is prepared to look after him for what would in effect be a trial period, there may be no need to make an interim care order, which is essentially a more intrusive order.

A key issue for the guardian in making this judgement would be the element of potential risk to the child. The court may make a direction regarding medical or psychiatric examination or other assessment of the child when it makes an interim care or interim supervision order (section 38(6)).

The guardian should consider the duration of orders desirable in each case. An initial order can be made for up to eight weeks but this should not be regarded as standard practice. Second or subsequent orders may last up to four weeks. Guardians should also address the question of reasonable contact during the duration of the order (See Children Act Guidance and Regulations Volume 1 — Court Orders, paragraphs 3.35–3.53).

Discharge of Care Orders and Discharge and Variation of Supervision Orders (section 39)

There is no provision in the Act for the variation of a care order. The Act assumes that the management of compulsory care is the responsibility of the local authority (see Children Act Guidance and Regulations Volume 1 — Court Orders, paragraph 3.54).

In applications to substitute a care order for a supervision order, guardians should note that a care order can only be made after a fresh finding that the conditions are satisfied, after a full hearing under section 31. In other words, the threshold criteria must be re-established.

The making of a section 8 residence order automatically discharges a care order and confers parental responsibility on the applicant. Guardians should be familiar with the Children and Young Persons Review of Children's Cases Regulations 1991 (Statutory Instrument No 895) which require the local authority to consider the discharge of the care order at every statutory review. Guardians should check that the discharge of the order has been actively considered.

The regulations also require that:

— at each review the child has to be informed of steps he may take himself, including applying to discharge the order, applying for a contact order, a variation of an existing contact order, for leave to apply for a residence order (section 10(8)), or the initiation of a complaint or representation under the procedures in section 26.

— the local authority should in suitable cases work towards bringing a care order to an end through rehabilitation of the child under section 23(6).

— the local authority should prepare for rehabilitation by advising, assisting and befriending him under section 24 and, if appropriate, encouraging and facilitating contacts under section 34.

The court may encourage the process of rehabilitation by varying the contact provisions consistent with a plan for return. Guardians therefore have a much wider range of options open to them in considering and planning for the child's return home through astute use of the available orders.

Young People Leaving Care

Where local authorities are applying to discharge care orders,guardians should consider the arrangements being made to offer assistance to that young person and the advice and befriending that they are likely to receive. Section 24 places a duty on local authorities to "advise, assist and befriend" young people leaving care. Assistance may be in kind or, in exceptional circumstances, in cash (section 24(7)).

Guardians should refer to the section on After Care in either Volume 3 or Volume 4 of the Children Act and Guidance and Regulations — It is unfortunate that young people leaving care are often required to "leave home"physically, financially, educationally and emotionally all on the same day in a way which would never be expected of a young person not in care.

Requirements of the Report under Part IV of the Children Act

— the report should be free-standing and capable of use as a reference point in subsequent proceedings.

— it should be disclosed seven days in advance of the hearing to Magistrates as well as to all parties. *There is no proof and report stage in care proceedings.* The aim of this is:

   * to allow all parties to see all the evidence well in advance; and

   * to allow the proceedings to become more inquisitorial rather than adversarial. It may well be that Magistrates will have reading time before the proceedings.

— the Report format (see Chapter 5) will be appropriate in most proceedings under Part IV. However, guardians should be flexible, since there will be cases in which specific headings are required and applications where a revised format (including a much shorter report) will be sufficient, e.g. applications to remove children in care from England and Wales.

Presentation of Guardian's Evidence

Guardians ad litem should be aware that the presentation of any new information, which may be instrumental in finding the conditions for a care or supervision order satisfied, should be discussed in advance with the child's solicitor to determine how best to handle the presentation of the evidence. It is not the guardian's responsibility to provide evidence on which to satisfy the conditions necessary for a care order.On the other hand they have a duty to notify the court of any facts relevant to the case, and should not wait until the final hearing to produce `rabbits from hats', as this may lead to unnecessary delay.

Sensitive Information

There may be exceptions to advance disclosure. Guardians should discuss this with their local courts and seek directions about how this is to be handled, for example — one of the parties may have HIV/AIDS or be terminally ill.

The Report and the Court Rules

The report must meet the Act's legal requirements. The Court Rules (Rule 11) state the guardian has the same responsibilities as the court to consider the requirements in section 1(2) (cutting down delay) and section 1(3)(a) to (f)(the welfare checklist).

— In practice the guardians are expected to make the welfare of the child paramount consideration in decision making.

— Guardians should consider the requirements of section 1(5), not to make an order unless that would be better than making no order at all.

— It is the responsibility of the guardian to advise the court on contact under section 34.

— The guardian must critically appraise the local authority plans for the child and their actions *in loco parentis*.

— The guardian's report should contain a separate section on section 1(3)(a), "the ascertainable wishes and feelings of the child concerned" (considered in the light of his age and understanding).

— The report should list the available options with a reasoned analysis of each to support the guardian's final recommendation. The exploration of the options should investigate the menu of orders available under the Act relevant to the case, either on their own or in different combinations.

Agreed Evidence

It is intended that, under the new system of advance disclosure and Directions Appointments, it will be possible to identify evidence agreed between the parties at a much earlier stage. However, it will be necessary for the guardian to check and report on matters which have already been agreed between the parties in order to ensure *firstly* that parents have understood clearly what it is they have agreed, and *secondly* that any agreement does not prejudice the welfare of the child (for example in a case where the local authority and the parents have agreed to the child's return home, but the guardian believes that the child is at risk). Under the Court Rules none of the parties may withdraw an application unless the guardian has been consulted and has had an opportunity to make representations to the Court (Rule 5).

The Child as a Witness

Section 96(1) and (2) of the Act provides that a child (if of sufficient age and understanding) may give unsworn evidence in civil proceedings provided he understands the need to speak the truth. Section 96(3)–(5) relaxes the `hearsay rule in relation to children in civil proceedings and would cover the introduction of video recordings of the child's evidence. The guardian and the child's solicitor will have to decide how to present the child's own evidence most effectively — this may include use of videoed material if adequate facilities are available (see also the Children Admissibility of Hearsay Evidence)Order 1991 Statutory Instrument No 1115).

While recent cases have illustrated the difficulties inherent in the giving of children's evidence, nevertheless the guardian should not underestimate the power of the child as a witness or their ability and desire to be involved directly in the court proceedings. It is, after all, the child who has experienced the events being discussed in court. It is too late to protect the child from these, but direct involvement in the determination of the case can help to enhance the child's sense of worth, and of being believed, and provide reassurance that the adult world is taking their distress seriously.

Contact

Central to the provisions of the Children Act is the assumption of reasonable contact which permeates all proceedings. Guardians should be familiar with the chapters in Volumes 3 and 4 of the Children Act Guidance and Regulations which deal with contact and build upon the guidance provided by the Code of Practice — Access to Children in Care which it replaces. They should also be familiar with the Children and Young Persons Contact with Children Regulations 1991 (Statutory Instrument No 891). Schedule 2 paragraph 15 of the Act deals with promotion and maintenance of contact between child and family. The concept of "contact" replaces that of access in previous legislation. In common with the rest of the proceedings under the Children Act 1989, contact becomes much more child-centred, and the concept of 'reasonable' contact will be a central issue in all cases in which guardians are involved.

There are two possible sorts of contact order available under the Act and the two should not be confused:

Firstly a section 8 contact order, which may be made in either public or private proceedings under the Act and which requires the person with whom the child is living to allow the child to visit or stay with the named person or to have contact with them.

Secondly a care contact order under section 34(5). This section assumes that there will be reasonable contact between a child and his family while the child is in care or the subject of any of the proceedings under Part v of the Act (Emergency Protection). The assumption of reasonable contact extends to children in police custody under section 46 and to children who are in secure accommodation under section 25.

The local authority also has a duty, under Part III of the Act, as part of its responsibility to attempt to maintain the child's family home, to promote contact between the child and his family if in their opinion it is necessary to do so in order to safeguard or promote his welfare (schedule 2 paragraph 10).

The local authority also has a responsibility to endeavour to promote contact between the child in accommodation and his parents, guardian or family under schedule 2 paragraphs 15 to 16.

Reasonable contact is not defined in the Act. Part of the guardian's role in determining the best interests of the child will be to advise the court about what reasonable contact would be for this particular child. If the guardian ad litem is aware that there are some very real logistical difficulties for the local authority in carrying out the court's recommendations in relation to contact then the guardian ad litem should be alert to these difficulties, while continuing to safeguard the right of the child to sustaining and comforting contacts with family and friends during a particularly stressful time of separation.

The guardian's recommendation for reasonable contact through any initial or interim stages of the proceedings should not necessarily be those that will stand for all time but should be reviewed at the time the guardian ad litem makes her final report and recommendation to the court, when she will be in a position to recommend the making of a section 8 contact order if this is appropriate.

Access/contact has been one of the most contentious of social work issues in recent years. Until January 1984 it was possible for a local authority to terminate a parent's access to a child as part of an internal administrative procedure. The assumption of reasonable contact is central to the concept of partnership with parents which is in turn central to the philosophy of the Act. It is perhaps the aspect of practice which will require the most adjustment on the part of both social work practitioners and guardians ad litem. The research findings of Millham et al showed how quickly relationships between children and families can deteriorate if contact is allowed to lapse, particularly in the early stages following the child's reception into care. The HASSASSA (Health and Social Services and Social Security Adjudications) Act 1983 legislation and the code of practice on access (which has been incorporated into the provisions of section 23(7) of the Act) have apparently had a limited effect on practice in relation to access/contact issues. Social work practitioners are divided amongst themselves on the situations in which contact should be terminated, and guardians will need to look at each case on the basis of the specific circumstances of the child.

Reasons for Contact:

— Contact may help a child to feel less rejected by his family;

— Contact may promote the child's adaptation to and feeling of security within the placement;

— Contact may promote the child's intellectual and emotional development;

— Contact may enable the child to develop a stable sense of self-identity and positive role models from members of his own race, culture or religion. (This will be particularly important for children who are trans-racially placed);

— Contact may enable the child to develop a realistic picture of his family.

Reasons for Termination or Refusal of Contact

— Where chronic and serious harm or distress may reasonably be attributed to existing contact arrangements;

— Where a child or young person persistently refuses to see his family;

— Where the parent or guardian concerned wilfully or persistently seeks to undermine the long-term planning for the child.

(Reproduced from a Summary by Guy Mitchell in "From Access to Contact", Panel News, Volume 4 Number 1 March 1991.)

Termination of Contact

Under section 34(6) the local authority may temporarily refuse reasonable contact if:

> "(a) they are satisfied that it is necessary to do so in order to safeguard or promote the child's welfare; and
>
> (b) the refusal
>
> > (i) is decided upon as a matter of urgency;
> >
> > (ii) does not last for more than seven days".

Under section 34(4) contact may be terminated by an application to the court either by the local authority or the child.

The success or failure of contact arrangements may well prove an accurate barometer of the state of the local authority's partnership with parents.

PROTECTION OF CHILDREN UNDER PART V OF THE ACT

Emergency Protection of Children

The prime social work duty is to protect the child from harm — not to provide evidence for criminal proceedings, for which the burden of proof is different and for which responsibility lies directly with the police.

In criminal proceedings

It must be "proved beyond reasonable doubt" that the alleged offence took place.

In care proceedings

The court must be satisfied that on "the balance of probability" the child requires protection, a weaker burden of proof than "beyond reasonable doubt". Therefore, although there may be a finding of "not guilty" in the criminal court, a civil court may still find the grounds for care proceedings satisfied.

Police powers

Police have an emergency power not available to other agencies to detain a child in a place of protection without prior application to the court. They can obtain a warrant under S.102 of the Children Act 1989 to enter premises and search for children in an emergency. They cannot also act without first obtaining a warrant, but in order to save life and limb they may enter premises under S.17(1)(e) of the Police and Criminal Evidence Act 1984.

Emergency protection orders (section 44)

In applications to challenge the making of emergency protection orders, guardians ad litem may be required to report to the court any time after seventy-two hours has elapsed and before the order expires after eight days. A direction made in connection with an emergency protection order can be challenged at any time (the order may be extended by a further seven days but no challenge is possible during that period). It is anticipated that most applications will be made without notice and will be ex-parte, with the leave of the Clerk, but applications may also be made in the presence of the parties. If parents attend the hearing at which the emergency protection order is made they lose their right to challenge the order subsequently. Hearings will require at least one day's notice. The eight day duration of the order does not include weekends or public holidays (i.e., eight "business days" — see Rule 1(2)). In cases of extreme urgency, and only with the leave of the Clerk to the Justices, it will be possible to make emergency applications by telephone and arrangements are contained in Court Rule 4(4).

Duty guardians

The demands of this new 'short-term' work requires that a guardian will be available at short notice, i.e. within 72 hours of the order being made, and will be flexible in pursuing the investigation during the days up to the hearing of the application. It is anticipated that guardians acting in this capacity will do so on the basis of arrangements to be worked out locally. It will not be necessary for guardians to attend the ex-parte applications, although attendance at a hearing where other parties are present would be a priority. It is desirable that, having once become involved in a case, the duty guardian should be able to carry on and see the case through to its conclusion in order to ensure continuity for the family, to avoid covering the same ground twice, and to provide the least confusion for the child concerned. However, in cases in which the duty guardian cannot continue to act, there should be a clear procedure for passing on relevant information and for clear messages to be given at the outset of the case to all concerned — the child, the family, the local authority and to foster and residential carers.

The Children Act Regulations and Guidance Volume 7 states that the court's expectations of the GALRO service at this initial stage are likely to be limited, but Panel Managers should clarify such expectations with the court clerks at the Family Proceedings Courts in their area. It is not considered necessary for there to be large numbers of Panel members on standby duty at any one time, but there will need to be an understood local procedure for guardians to be contacted at very short notice. Guardians may also be appointed at short notice in other proceedings, for example applications under section 31 where the local authority is requesting an interim order at the first hearing, and in applications for Secure Accommodation Orders under Section 25.

Challenges to the making of emergency protection orders

The guardian should cover, at least, the following points:

— examine the circumstances which led to the order being made;

— form an opinion about whether or not the emergency is continuing, i.e. would the court consider that there is *"reasonable cause to believe the child concerned is likely to suffer significant harm if the order is not extended"?* (section 45(5)

— provide information to the court on the position of the child and the child's wishes and feelings;

— be in a position to ask questions of local authority witnesses. If, exceptionally, no solicitor has been appointed, the guardian should be in a position to ask questions directly of local authority witnesses;

— check that the possibility of reducing the risk by removing the person believed to pose that risk to the child has been considered;

— provide the court with an assessment of the extended family's capacity to protect the child if the order is discharged and the situation at home is still in doubt;

— provide a clear recommendation to the court, bearing in mind that the first priority is the safety of the child;

— advise the court about the child's contacts. These are not the arrangements that must stand for all time, but are those which will best meet the needs of the child at a time of extreme insecurity, confusion and distress. The guardian should also pay particular attention to maintaining contact with siblings and grandparents;

— advise the court as to whether there is a need for any directions or assessment.

Oral evidence

Because of the time constraints, guardians may be giving evidence orally at this stage rather than risking delay by preparing a written report. Clearly, a brief written report will always be helpful to the court, but the lack of it should not be a reason for adjournment.

Child Assessment Order (Section 43)

Child assessment orders are completely new and have no parallel in previous legislation. They are aimed at a specific situation in which there is reasonable cause to suspect that the child is suffering or is likely to suffer significant harm, an assessment of the child is required to determine this and it is unlikely an assessment will be made or be satisfactory in the absence of an order. Only the court can authorise the child's removal from home, and make directions as to the nature and manner of the assessment to be carried out. A child assessment order can last for a maximum of seven days.

Guardians should be aware that the threshold criteria is one of suspicion of suffering or likelihood of suffering significant harm, which is a lower criteria of belief than that required for an emergency protection order. The order therefore lowers the level of state intervention into family life, so particular care must be taken to ensure that any assessment should provide maximum information with minimum disruption to the child. Children will not be removed from home for any period within the order unless the court so directs. If the guardian believes after hearing the application for the child assessment order, that an emergency protection order is appropriate, she should make this alternative recommendation to the court. However, the child assessment order does not have to be activated on the day it is granted. The court may state the day from which it is to take effect so that it coincides with medical and psychiatric appointments.

Judgements about what assessments are necessary or desirable are extremely complex. What would happen, for example, if a court directed that the child should have a biopsy in order to diagnose a medical problem and the child refused? One underlying principle in such cases must be that the outcome for the child will be considerably improved if all the professionals concerned communicate fully and liaise effectively on the best means of acquiring any necessary information, while incurring the least distress for the child concerned.

The guardian should explore with the child his reasons for refusing any assessment, but should take particular care to avoid coercing the child into agreement, even where there is a belief that the refusal to comply is itself the product of coercion by a parent, relative or friend.

In covering at least the following points, guardians should:

— decide if the order is appropriate or whether an emergency protection order is necessary;

— satisfy themselves and the court about the applicant's precise plans as to how the assessment is to be made, whether medical, social work, psychological or psychiatric; when and where it will take place; who will carry it out and how; and if the assessment is necessary;

— ascertain whether or not the child is prepared to give consent to such assessments or examinations and ensure that the child has the necessary information on which to base such a consent;

— advise the court about the child's capacity to make an informed decision regarding consent to assessment;

— satisfy themselves about the arrangements for contact during the period of the assessment if, exceptionally, the court directs the child's removal from home;

— give a clear recommendation to the court about whether or not the application should be granted and if it is whether any additional court directions would be appropriate;

— advise the court in relation to the child's attendance at court;

— clarify arrangements whereby the court is advised on the outcome of the assessment if no further application is made.

Specified Proceedings

By virtue of section 41(6)(i) and Court Rule 2(2), there are four additional types of proceedings specified where the guardian ad litem may be appointed:

Applications for Secure Accommodation Orders (Section 25)

Guardians should be familiar with the Children (Secure Accommodation) Regulations 1991 (Statutory Instrument No 1505), The Children (Secure Accommodation) (No 2) Regulations 1991 (Statutory Instrument No 2034) and Chapter 8 of the Children Act Guidance and Regulations Volume 4 — Residential Care, which deals with secure accommodation. They should refer in particular to Chapter 5 of Volume 1 of the Children Act Guidance and Regulations — Court Orders, which deals with secure accommodation orders. The main changes include the extension of the secure accommodation provisions to children accommodated by health or local authorities or National Health Service Trusts, or in residential care, nursing or mental nursing homes.

This constitutes a completely new area of work for guardians ad litem who may become involved in secure accommodation for the first time. The legal and ethical issues involved in the placement of children in secure accommodation are different from those involved in the guardian's other duties under the Act. However, the same skills and approaches are required. The guardian ad litem's role is to advise the court about the best interests of the child. It could be argued that placing young people in secure units is sometimes more about containment and control than about best interests. However, it is appropriate that young people, faced with the prospect of placement to secure accommodation, should have somebody to provide an independent view and assessment of all the circumstances surrounding the case. The involvement of the guardian, working with the solicitor on behalf of the child, should ensure a careful scrutiny of the facts of the case. In these types of cases the child has a statutory right to legal representation by a solicitor of his own choosing. Regardless of the guardian's possible views about containment being in that child's best interest, the child may disagree when faced with the prospect of placement in secure accommodation.

There are two routes into secure accommodation. Children and young people may enter by either the criminal or the civil route. Guardians will only be involved in the civil route.

"Where reference is made to applications being made to the 'court' for authority to keep a child in secure accommodation, this means a juvenile or magistrates' court, as appropriate where the child is the subject of criminal proceedings (i.e., remand to local authority accommodation). In all other cases, applications are made to the family proceedings court unless the matter arises in the context of a case already before a County or High Court, in which case applications should be made to that court. In addition to a child's entitlement to be legally represented when applications to restrict liberty are being considered by any court, children appearing before a civil or magistrates' court for such purposes will be entitled to have a guardian ad litem appointed to safeguard their interests". (Paragraph 8.4, Regulations and Guidance Volume 4 — Residential Care.)

Local authority responsibility for children in secure accommodation

As far as possible, placement in secure accommodation should form part of the general local authority plan for the child, and should not occur as a reaction to a particular crisis. In placing the child, the local authority must have regard to their general duty under section 22, including the duty to safeguard and promote the child's welfare (section 22(3) (a)) and, so far as reasonably practicable, to ascertain the wishes and feelings regarding the matter of the child, his parents and any other person whose wishes and feelings they consider relevant (section 22(4)).

Regulation 14 of the Children (Secure Accommodation) Regulations 1991 requires local authorities to inform -

— parents;

— any person with parental responsibility;

— the child's independent visitor, if one has been appointed;

— any other person who they consider should be informed;

if a child to whom section 25 of the Act applies is kept in secure accommodation in a community home, and it is intended to make an application to keep the child in that accommodation.

Outside the court processes, guardians should also note that Regulation 15 requires local authorities to appoint at least three persons, at least one of whom must not be employed by the local authority, who shall review the keeping of the child in secure accommodation for the

Subject to any direction made under section 91(14), in general section 91(15) and (17) preclude a fresh application being made before six months has elapsed unless the court gives leave.

Chapter 7

Working with Children

THE GUARDIAN/CHILD RELATIONSHIP

It is hard for children and young people to appreciate the nuances of relationship implicit in the tasks of social worker, educational clinical psychologist, child psychiatrist or guardian ad litem. Most children are extremely patient and forbearing about the introduction of yet another strange person into their already fragmented lives but in this context guardians are in control and must plan their involvement with the child in a way which keeps additional stress and anxiety to an absolute minimum. Children, like adults, appreciate honesty in all their transactions and can forgive almost anything more easily than being told lies or being misled. They are also realists. It may be that the final outcome of the guardian's involvement will not be the one that the child would have preferred. On the other hand, if the process of decision making has involved listening to the child and treating him with respect and honesty, then the child will emerge at the end of the court proceedings knowing that at least he has been listened to, has been recognised and valued as an individual and has participated in the making of a decision which is a working synthesis of what is best for him, what is possible and what he would have liked to happen.

The difficulty of striking the right balance in this complex task should not be under-estimated. Throughout the process the guardian ad litem is seeking to acquire enough information to represent the child effectively, without becoming over-involved, and to establish a rapport with the child without raising unreal expectations of an ongoing relationship.

Confidentiality

The limits of the guardian's confidentiality should be made clear to the child from the beginning of the guardian's contact.

Guardians should ensure that they always see the child alone in a situation in which the child feels at ease, and which offers privacy. The only exception to this rule would be if the child was violent, or the guardian went to see the child specifically in order to introduce a specialist expert witness or an interpreter. Regulation 7(3) and (5) of the Children's Homes Regulations 1991 requires local authorities to provide suitable facilities for any child accommodated within a children's home to meet privately with his guardian ad litem and to provide access to a telephone where the child can make and receive private calls.

The Limits of the Guardian's Involvement

The guardian ad litem is appointed for the purpose of specific court proceedings in relation to the child and the time-limited, task-centred nature of the role must be clearly reflected in the direct work carried out with the child. The role is essentially information-gathering, not therapeutic. For this reason a guardian must avoid allowing a dependency relationship to develop or encouraging this via the use of inappropriate techniques or styles of intervention, even if the guardian is aware that the child has a need for counselling and ongoing work which is not being met elsewhere. Children will usually have their own social worker who is responsible for the ongoing work with them. The role of the guardian should be to alert the appropriate agencies and workers to any deficiencies and to make a clear statement to the court about the child's current state of development, knowledge and understanding. On the other hand, guardians cannot simply abandon children to their fate, but must use their considerable powers, within the parameters of the appointment by the court, to ensure not only that attention is focused on the child's needs but that those needs are met. For example, the guardian may arrange a contact visit between parent and child if this has not been done in order to assess the interaction between them. This should only be done in consultation with the local authority social workers who are responsible for the case. The Children Act gives guardians an extremely broad remit to act on behalf of children and this should be fully explored.

The purpose of the guardian ad litem's involvement with the child is:

Firstly to provide the court with as full and accurate an assessment of the child's life and functioning as possible, in order that the court may make an order which will meet the child's needs as appropriately as possible, bearing in mind all the circumstances of the case.

Secondly to fulfil the duty to ascertain the child's wishes and feelings and to ensure that the court is aware of them in making any decision about the child's future.

Observation and Assessment

Guardians will find it helpful in this context to read the Department of Health publication "Protecting Children—A Guide for Social Workers undertaking a Comprehensive Assessment" (HMSO 1988) and the Report of the Inquiry into Child Sexual Abuse in Cleveland. Making an accurate assessment of a child's needs at a particular point is done not just by observation which is a passive activity, but by interpreting the material observed with a high degree of accuracy. This is the essential social work skill and it is the core of the guardian's task. Information on which to base an assessment comes from the careful collation of material both from the child and from informed others, i.e. involved professionals, relatives and carers.

The Child

Careful observation of children in different situations, and of their interaction with others, is an important pre-requisite of assessment. How the child looks is a significant indication of state of mind and mental and physical well-being. The guardian ad litem will wish to see the child with the natural parent or parents, with foster carers or in the child's home, at school and with siblings. If possible, observations should be recorded simply without accompanying interpretation. Interpretation comes later with the guardian's assessment and conclusions. Much greater weight should be given to detailed observation and carefully collected and recorded evidence. Generalised statements and ill-founded assumptions must be challenged. The consequences of relying on personal values, making false assumptions or ignoring or distorting evidence can be very serious for the child. The implications of the research findings on current decision making are that all professionals involved in child care decisions would benefit from some rigorous training in the collection and use of evidence and should be challenged to examine the values on which their views are based (see: Patterns and Outcomes in Child Placement, HMSO 1991).

Sources Other than the Child

The guardian ad litem will also wish to be aware of any particular skills, talents, pre-occupations or idiosyncrasies that the child possesses as all of these things will be part of the child's unique personality. Here the school or nursery will have a major contribution to make. The facilitation of the child's development in a particular area of interest or ability (e.g. a talent for music or a sport) may be a significant factor in making a recommendation for the child's future and helpful for the child's acceptance of the decision reached.

On the basis of the information gained from these sources, either through interviews or through the study of written reports, the guardian ad litem should have accurate knowledge about the child's mental, physical and emotional development including any particular health problems, or areas of disability. She should know, for example, whether a baby or toddler has reached the milestones appropriate to his age and whether he is up to date with his programme of injections.

Percentile Charts

The guardian should check that the child's current weight and height are accurately recorded on a percentile chart. Percentile charts are a device for measuring the physical development of a particular child against a normal child of the same age. Percentile charts should be filled in regularly and not just at crisis points in a child's life. They are only meaningful if the child has been weighed on accurately balanced scales wearing the same amount of clothing on each occasion taking into account the time of the child's last meal. In all cases percentile charts require careful interpretation in the light of full knowledge of the child's psycho-social background.

Medical Records

Guardians do not have a statutory right of access to medical records. However, there is a great deal of valuable information in medical records which is generally under-used, or not amalgamated with social workers records to provide a comprehensive picture. Guardians do have the right of access to any medical records stored as part of the social services file, and should bear in mind that 'medical histories of children in care are usually grossly inadequate and seldom include an interview with the parents' (Patterns and Outcomes in Child Placement).

Key Elements in Assessment

Bonding and attachment

In the last two decades particular attention has been focused on the importance of bonding and attachment in making decisions about children's future care.

Definition of attachment

Attachment is an affectionate bond between two individuals that endures through space and time and serves to join them emotionally' (Kennell 1976). Attachments `help a child to`attain his full potential, sort out what he perceives, think logically, develop a conscience, become self-reliant, cope with stresses and frustration, handle fear and worry, develop future relationships and reduce jealousy' (V. Fahlberg 1982).

Attachment describes a natural two way process between carer and child. It is the carer's committed and central interest in a particular child who has a special meaning for him or her that assists healthy psychological growth. Separation or loss of the person to whom the child is attached can lead to traumatic emotional reactions of grief, mourning and anger in both the carer and the child.

This is often not fully understood or acknowledged at the point of removal from the family, and can destroy the trust between the child and the helping agencies.

Secure and insecure attachment

Attachments may be secure or insecure. Insecurely attached children who have been abused may paradoxically cling to the abusing or neglecting parent but this is not a sign of good and secure attachment. The insecurely attached child may form indiscriminate relationships with adults and again this is not a good sign. A child who is reluctant to leave the object of their attachment may be exhibiting an insecure rather than a secure bond—much depends on the keenness and accuracy of the guardian's assessment in determining the nature and extent of the attachment. It is also important to understand that the bonding of a child with an adult is not something that happens immediately. It takes place over time and will be subject to peaks and troughs.

A child with secure attachments will have a safe base from which to explore the world, and will learn to cope effectively and confidently with new people and situations. Guardians can obtain much valuable information from younger children by observing them with different people and in different aspects of their environment.

In the course of their investigation, guardians will want to know about the people to whom the `child is, and has been, attached, in particular where the primary attachment now lies (whether that is to a mother, father, older sibling or foster carer). There may be key attachments to people who have no recognised role in the child's life, e.g. a neighbour or friend or the school dinner lady, who may be one of the few consistently kind people in the child's life. Bonds of affection are resilient in that, once made, they do not necessarily require reciprocation from the object of the affection. Children and young people are intensely loyal and so, even when their parents may not "deserve" their continuing affection, the attachment may continue.

Disruption of the child's key attachment causes profound distress to the child, particularly for young children and babies between the ages of six months and three years. Multiple disruptions undermine the child's capacity to make meaningful and secure relationships with adults and other children. It is a sad fact that some children do experience a shocking number of changes of carers, both in and out of "care". Guardians may find it helpful to prepare a disruption chart showing the child's age and number of changes of carer, as this can be a powerful illustration to the courts of the fragmented life of a particular child. The guardian ad litem should look at the chart to consider how much more disruption this child can take (see example at the end of this Chapter).

Identity

As a child grows older, questions of identity, of belonging to a particular family and to a wider community, become increasingly important.

An awareness of individual, familial, racial and cultural heritage is an aspect of development which has perhaps not been given sufficient prominence. In recent years the recognition of the importance of "permanence" in children's lives, combined with the diminishing resources available for preventive work with families, has led to an over-emphasis on substitute care as the preferred "permanent" solution. Core identity should be looked at alongside key attachments in making any plan for the child's future. Guardians should be aware of the child's understanding of his origins and the importance of that identity for that particular child. Children in both residential and long term foster care may have very little idea or knowledge of their background on which to shape their identity and yet the birth family may in fact be the most stable influence in the child's life, even if actual contact is very limited. Children in long term foster care often have no knowledge of their parents' hair-colouring, facial characteristics, personality traits or medical history. Sadly, foster parents are often not in possession of this knowledge either, so are not able to reinforce the child's attempts to understand his origins. A child who does not know anything about his background may be anonymous in his own eyes and may suffer from poor self esteem and confusion. If there is something "secret" or "bad" about his past, how can he be "good"? The child's state of knowledge and understanding about their genetic, racial, cultural, and emotional inheritance should be a key factor in the guardian's assessment. Although records have sometimes been scant in the past, hopefully there will be better opportunities in future for children to piece together their own histories.

WORKING WITH CHILDREN

Children in Minority Ethnic Eroups

Children must be recognised within the context of their race, culture, language and religion. Jasmine Beckford was a black child whose social worker was Swedish, the health visitor was Chinese, the supervisor American, the family Afro-Caribbean and the foster parent, Anglo-Indian. Cross cultural factors can have a profound influence on assessment, decision making and collaborative work amongst professionals and guardians ad litem should be particularly aware of this in their work. "The most outstanding finding about minority ethnic children in public care is the grossly disproportionate number of those of mixed racial parentage" (Patterns and Outcomes in Child Placement, HMSO 1991, page 15). *Bebbington and Miles* found that such children were two and a half times as likely to enter care as white children. Sadly there are very few guardians from ethnic minorities currently on panels. It will be necessary to ensure that panel members have access to cross cultural consultation and to appropriate interpreters if necessary. They should not rely on the good offices of the child's friends or relatives, who may have their own particular values and perspective on the case.

Ascertaining the Child's Wishes and Feelings

The guardian should be clear from an early stage about whether this is a child who is able to express his wishes and feelings. This will depend not just on whether the child is old enough but whether he is free enough from disturbance or disability. Some guardians have embarked on lengthy and time-consuming work with children involving complicated techniques of communication, before recognising that the child is not of an age or understanding to express his wishes and feelings. Some people are better trained than others to communicate with children and legions of Fisher Price play people or other props will not make a great deal of difference. Guardians should be realistic about what they can aim to achieve within the time span of their involvement with the child and, most importantly, they should be clear with the child about how that work is to be carried out. Bear in mind that the relationship with the child is not an end in itself but a means of informing the court of the child's present situation and current state of mind. Do not underestimate the value of a straightforward and honest conversation with the child.

WORKING WITH YOUNGER CHILDREN

Many guardians have developed creative techniques for indirect work with younger children. Some carry toy boxes to enable children to engage in play. Drawing, painting and the use of model families, homes and court scenes are all useful tools to facilitate communication.

> **Play "Kit"**—A basic "kit" for guardians might include the following:
>
> *Pipe cleaner dolls*—Small enough to be easily handled by young children.
>
> *Pads of A4 drawing paper.*
>
> *Coloured crayons or pencils.*
>
> *A dinky car and truck*—Useful to describe journeys and changes.
>
> *Anti-colouring books*—Helps children to look at their hopes, fears and fantasies by using imaginative colouring material. (Available from Bookstall Services; Anti-Colouring Books by Susan Striker and Edward Kimmel, Published Hippo Books Scholastic Publications Ltd, London.)

Materials should be kept as simple as possible to avoid overwhelming and confusing the child with unaccustomed toys. With very young children the observed evidence, e.g. in attachment, may be strong enough for the guardian to give an opinion about the child's feelings even though the child is not able to express them. Care should be taken to state upon what the opinion is based.

Interpreting the Material

The guardian's skill lies in making the correct interpretation of information gained through play. Here the diagnostic tool is *the guardian*, not the playbox. Great care should be exercised in interpreting children's drawing, and guardians should beware of projecting their own interpretations onto the child's drawing. The guardian can help the child to make connections but should guard against:

    (a)   leading questions;

    (b)   projecting her own thoughts and feelings into the child's interpretation;

    (c)   controlling rather than facilitating the interview;

    (d)   believing that her efforts will always achieve a clear conclusion.

The guardian should be able to give the child a sense of security in the interview without inhibiting spontaneous interaction. If the interview is to open-ended the child may feel confused. The guardian should make the situation clear, e.g. how long the interview is expected to last. Although guardians should avoid leading the child in a particular direction, general facilitative statements are helpful, e.g. "lots of children would feel just like you in your situation," rather than "I think you're saying that ..." etc. It will also reduce the burden on the child if guardians have tested out as much of the evidence as they can indirectly before approaching delicate matters directly with the child.

Reports should take care to differentiate between observed fact and opinion. Writing or drawings produced by the child should be attached to the report and clearly marked with the date and the circumstances in which they were produced.

WORKING WITH OLDER CHILDREN

Older children and teenagers often find it tremendously reassuring to know that there is somebody there specifically for them during the traumatic period leading up to the court proceedings. If they are able to see the guardian as a channel of communication between themselves and the court, they may well experience the relationship as an empowering one, enabling them to participate in the decisions being made about their lives.

The work should be planned carefully with the child at an early stage. The guardian should *stick to any arrangements* made with the child so he knows exactly when and how often he will be seen. Direct transactions between the guardian and the child should be clear and informative, starting with introductions and explanations of why the guardian is there. Do not assume that this will already have been done by others. Above all the guardian should be honest, give the child the information necessary to make an informed decision about important matters and discuss the conduct of the case with him.

For example:

(a) giving consent to medical or other examinations;

(b) deciding whether or not to attend court;

(c) undertaking receipt of the documents served by the court;

(d) discussing any contacts the child may wish to maintain or make;

(e) ensuring that the child understands that it is the court who will make the final decision;

(f) determining whether or not there are specific people that the child wishes the guardian to interview.

Guardians should recognise that there is a tension inherent in their responsibility to put a view to the court about the child's best interest while, at the same time, making sure that the child's wishes and feelings are given appropriate prominence. However, a successful working relationship can result in a strong and effective partnership which incorporates the child's wishes without sacrificing any of his interests. This can be the most satisfying aspect of the guardian's work.

Children's Evidence

Section 96 relaxes the rules of evidence in favour of children to allow hearsay and unsworn evidence to be heard. In some cases the Court of Appeal has requested that, in order to be fair to all parties, children's evidence, particularly in relation to the disclosure of sexual abuse, should be videoed. Clearly guardians cannot control, nor would wish to inhibit, children's spontaneous conversation which may reveal unsuspected abuse and which may not be videoed. In such cases the child's testimony should be clearly and carefully noted at the time and submitted to the court and to the local authority. However, guardians will usually be aware of the possibility or suspicion of abuse from the background information available to them and should be in a position to solicit such information in a controlled, secure and neutral interviewing environment. Guardians may wish to investigate the possibility of videoing an interview with the child if the proper facilities are available. Such recordings may:

(a) enhance the child's chance of providing acceptably hard evidence, or indication of abuse;

(b) give parents or others the opportunity to see and challenge the evidence in context;

(c) allow the content of the interview to be critically evaluated;

(d) relieve the child of the distressing necessity to repeat evidence in additional interviews.

In this way misunderstandings and further pressure on the child may be kept to a minimum. Guardians should always ask the child's permission before videoing an interview—to do so without the child's knowledge would be an abuse of trust.

Guardians may find it helpful to read Chapter 11 in The Evidence of Children—The Law and the Psychology by J R Spencer and Rhona Flin (Blackstone 1990) for a discussion of the differences between open-ended, leading and facilitative questions.

The Criminal Justice Act 1991 and the recommendations of the Pigot Committee (as partially adopted) will substantially change the position of children giving evidence in criminal proceedings. In particular, the Act seeks to ensure that any child who wishes to give evidence can do so. The question of competence to give evidence is no longer related to age, with the possibility that children as young as five or six will be directly involved in court proceedings. A major improvement will be to make video recordings admissible as evidence in chief, provided the child is available for cross-examination at the trial.

INTER-PROFESSIONAL WORKING

The guardian should be alert to opportunities to co-operate with the child's social worker and other professionals in observing and assessing children. Where there are facilities to see the child through a one-way mirror, the guardian may wish to observe the child's interview with another professional rather than subject the child to additional interviews which cover the same ground. This in no way absolves the guardian of the responsibility to see the child alone but this approach should be considered within the overall planning.

If, during the course of the guardian's contact with the child, the child discloses hitherto unknown facts about physical or sexual abuse, the guardian should alert the local authority social worker in order that the correct child abuse procedures may be initiated. It is not part of the guardian's task to carry out "disclosure" work, although this is in itself a misnomer as it supposes that there is something to disclose.

If the guardian is of the opinion that the child is in need of longer term therapeutic intervention, then the local authority should be informed of this in order to make the necessary arrangements.

Working with Young People Leaving Care

Guardians involved with young people leaving care should be familiar with the provisions of section 24 which require local authorities to 'advise, assist and befriend young people.' There is no direct duty on local authorities to provide a grant to enable a young person to embark on independent living. Guardians should consider the position of the young person leaving care, bearing in mind that physical, emotional and financial maturity do not take place simultaneously on a child's sixteenth birthday. It may be that discharging the order would be worse for the child than allowing the order to continue—an interesting variation on the provisions of section 1(5). Clearly much will depend on the young person's wishes in the matter, but this particular group of children are in a very vulnerable position.

> *"leaving care for independence is a crisis which brings to the surface past deficits in care and attainment; it often requires but does not receive a major input of services and support"*
> (Patterns and Outcomes in Child Placements)

Children under the Children Act 1989 are supported by a sound legislative framework and a comprehensive infrastructure of regulations and guidance which cover virtually all aspects of child care policy and practice. Together they provide an opportunity for good professional practice which should be fully used and explored by guardians in their work with and on behalf of children.

Chapter 9 of Volume 3 and Chapter 7 of Volume 4—Children Act Guidance and Regulations deal with after care advice and assistance. Voluntary organisations should also help prepare a young person for independent living, which it is suggested should include planning in conjunction with all other interested parties, e.g. education and housing authorities, health authorities and where appropriate other local authorities. The provisions of section 27 may be helpful in this context with its encouragement of co-operation between authorities.

Children with Disabilities

The definition of children in need contained in section 17 of the Children Act 1989 includes children who have disabilities and who, for the purposes of Act, are defined as children who are—blind, deaf, or dumb or who suffer from mental disorder of any kind or who are substantially and permanently handicapped by illness, injury, or congenital deformity, or such other disability as may be prescribed.

Sensitivity will be required in making an accurate assessment of each child with a disability. Guardians should seek the advice of colleagues and consultants with experience relevant to the needs of individual children. They should also refer to Volume 6 of the guidance and regulations—'Children with Disabilities'.

'the range of duties and powers provided in Part III of the Act should therefore be seen as an important opportunity not only to ensure that children with disabilities are treated as children first, but also to ensure access to the range of generic and specialist provision available to support children and families in their own homes and their local communities'. (Paragraph 3.3).

DISCLOSURE AND DENIAL

Guidelines for interviews with children

(Cleveland Inquiry Report, Paragraph 12.34).

1. It is undesirable to call interviews "disclosure interviews", which precludes the notion that sexual abuse might not have occurred.

2. All interviews should be undertaken only by those with some training experience and aptitude for talking with children.

3. The interview should be approached with an open mind.

4. The style of the interview should be open-ended questions to support and encourage the child in free recall.

5. There should be, where possible, only one and not two interviews for the purpose of evaluation and interviews should not be too long.

6. The adult should go at the pace of the child and not of the adult.

7. The setting for the interview must be suitable and sympathetic.

8. It must be accepted that, at the end of the interview, the child may have no information to support the suspicion of sexual abuse and the position will remain unclear.

9. There must be careful recording of the interview and what the child says, whether or not there is a video recording.

10. It must be recognised that the use of selective techniques makes great difficulties in subsequent court proceedings.

11. Adequate training for those engaged in this work is of great importance.

12. A facilitative interview should be treated as a second stage.

INVOLVING CHILDREN IN DECISION MAKING

Check-list

* Make sure that the child has accurate and necessary information on which to make an informed decision e.g. re medical or other assessment.

* Bear in mind the child's developmental and emotional state which will dictate much of the decision making and which will affect the extent to which he will be able to be involved in conciliation.

* Be prepared to go at the child's pace, if at all possible, allow him to influence the agenda and to change his mind on reflection but make it clear that it is the court who makes the final decision.

* Consult and inform the child at each stage of the decision making.

* Ensure that the child knows what options are:

    — available;

    — realistic; and

    — desirable

e.g. Does the child know that his parents/siblings/ grandparents wish to see him? Who does he wish to see?

* Ensure that the child is not left alone with the responsibility for making decisions which may be irreversible e.g. Is the child saying he does not want to maintain links with his family of origin because he does not want to hurt or alienate loved foster parents who are the basis of his present security?

* Keep the choices for the child as open and flexible as possible for as long as possible, e.g.: consistent schooling (particularly in the early years and between the ages of fourteen and eighteen); access to positive role models of the same race, culture, language and religion.

* Allow the child time and the opportunity to challenge decisions as they are made.

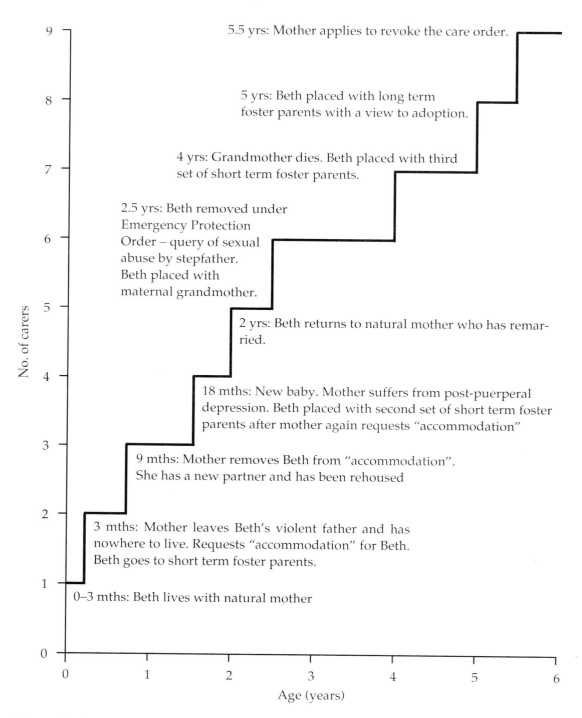

Disruption chart
Beth, aged five and a half.

5.5 yrs: Mother applies to revoke the care order.

5 yrs: Beth placed with long term
foster parents with a view to adoption.

4 yrs: Grandmother dies. Beth placed with third
set of short term foster parents.

2.5 yrs: Beth removed under
Emergency Protection
Order – query of sexual
abuse by stepfather.
Beth placed with
maternal grandmother.

2 yrs: Beth returns to natural mother who has remarried.

18 mths: New baby. Mother suffers from post-puerperal
depression. Beth placed with second set of short term foster
parents after mother again requests "accommodation"

9 mths: Mother removes Beth from "accommodation".
She has a new partner and has been rehoused

3 mths: Mother leaves Beth's violent father and has
nowhere to live. Requests "accommodation" for Beth.
Beth goes to short term foster parents.

0–3 mths: Beth lives with natural mother

No. of carers

Age (years)

Having had eight different carers before her mother applied to revoke the care order, can this
child tolerate the risk of further disruption?

*In some cases change can be positive. A child may be removed from a situation of risk. Some races and
cultures have a broader concept of the extent of a family, which may encompass frequent changes of
carers. Far from having a negative effect, this may increase the child's feeling of security within his
community.*

Chapter 8

Working with Parents and Carers

"Research shows that partnership with parents has not been integral to past or current social work practice. Some fundamental changes in attitude will be required if the spirit of the new Act is to be fully implemented" (Patterns and Outcomes in Child Placement, HMSO 1991).

It is extremely common for parents to say to guardians that they do not understand why their child is in care, nor what they have to do to satisfy the local authority that they are fit parents for the child. This is partly because limited social work resources tend to follow the child so work with parents may cease once the child comes into care. One of the guardian's first tasks, therefore, is to ensure that parents understand the legal proceedings in which the child and they themselves are involved and why those proceedings have been initiated by the local authority. They should also be clear about their full party status in all proceedings, their right to separate legal representation and their eligibility for legal aid. The Court Rules lay a responsibility on the guardian to ensure that parents (in common with any other interested parties) are informed of their eligibility to be joined in any proceedings. While the legal representation of children has improved considerably since the establishment of the Panels, parents' legal representation can be of a lesser quality. This is usually because parents are not aware of the existence of child care law solicitors.

PARTNERSHIP WITH PARENTS

Working in partnership with parents is not always easy. "The concept of parental responsibilty or recognition that parents by virtue of being a parent have rights and duties that endure throughout childhood. These must be recognised by those who provide services for children and their families, and their existence should fundamentally shift the flawed practice that research revealed during the 1980's." Jo Tunnard—Family Rights Group. However, any parent who has a child in care, particularly one whose child has been removed in an emergency, is often suffering from shock at the trauma of what has occurred as well as grief and loss about the child's removal. Parents may also be awaiting the outcome of police investigations and be in a state of acute anxiety and despair. It is at the point of reception to care that relationships between the local authority, parents and the extended family can go badly wrong. It is important for the guardian to understand the state of those relationships and how they have come about, as this will inform her interpretation of the parents' attitudes and actions.

The Act assumes that, in general, families have the capacity to cope with their own problems. Some families, however, reach a stage where they are not able to resolve their own difficulties and are therefore providing inadequate care for their child. They may look to social services for support and assistance. If they do this the emphasis on partnership and support should mean that they receive a positive response which reduces any fears they may have of stigma or loss of parental responsibility. Social work input should aim at identifying and providing for the child's needs rather than focusing on parental shortcomings in a negative manner.

Written agreements are essential for partnership work and guardians should examine all correspondence including agreements between parents and local authorities. Whether or not the parents have attended reviews and case conferences is also an indication of to what extent partnership' has existed.

PARENTS AND CARERS AND THE GUARDIAN

Most parents welcome the independent involvement of the guardian and, provided the role is clearly explained to them, will put considerable faith in the outcome of the guardian's investigations. Very few parents refuse to see the guardian—on the contrary, most are anxious to have an opportunity to put their point of view. A guardian should always ask parents for a list of people who they would wish her to see. These people may have little to add to the case, but at least the parents will feel that the guardian has listened and followed up every avenue possible in a fair and even-handed manner. It is very important that parents see the guardian as providing an independent view. If they feel that the view is biased or that the guardian is controlled by the local authority which has removed their child they will have little faith in, or acceptance of, the final recommendation. If, on the other hand, they feel that the guardian has been fair and honest in her dealings with them, they will be much more inclined to accept the reality of what she is saying and to understand why she is making the final recommendation, even if that recommendation does not include the return of the child.

The guardian should ensure, therefore, that parents know what evidence is to be adduced and that they are aware of the local authority and the guardian's case before the final disclosure of the reports. The difference between criminal and civil burdens of proof must be clearly explained to parents if they are to be helped to accept the outcome of a hearing. Remember that partnership with parents does not mean collusion with parents or a shift in emphasis away from child protection as a primary objective. It does mean using the personal and material resources of the social services department to enable parents to discharge their responsibilities to their children in an appropriate and positive manner.

CHILDREN BEING ACCOMMODATED (SECTION 20)

The change of emphasis in the Act provided by the provision of accommodation for children, replaces section 2 of the Child Care Act 1980 and provides a concept of shared care rather than statutory intervention. The emphasis on keeping families together through the provision of the range of services to support families and children in need, outlined in Part III, should diminish the need to take children into long term compulsory care. The new arrangements should be seen as more akin to short term "respite" care than the old voluntary care. The provision of accommodation reinforces the need to support parents in carrying out their responsibilities rather than taking those responsibilities away from them and applies equally to children with disabilities and those in need of protection.

The Act requires a change of culture and a clear differentiation between voluntary and statutory arrangements. The fact that parents no longer have to give notice of removal from accommodation worries some social workers who fear that children in accommodation will be at the mercy of parents who may act on whim. It also provides foster parents who offer accommodation to children less control over the day to day aspects of the lives of children in their care. Guardians will wish to gain experience of the new arrangements, which will require:

— a change in culture on the part of local authorities and foster parents;

— the use of partnership agreements and written contracts between parents, foster parents and local authorities;

— a review of arrangements for ending the accommodation.

At the end of the day, the local authority's final sanction will lie in the ability to initiate statutory proceedings but much will depend on an appreciation that this is a new service with a new ethos, not just a new Act.

The Assumption of Reasonable Contact

Under section 34 the local authority is required to make an arrangement for reasonable contact between parent and child. Guardians will wish to discuss these arrangements with the parents or carers and may wish to observe contact meetings if this is appropriate. Schedule 2, paragraph 15 of the Act deals with questions relating to the promotion and maintenance of contact between child and family, both for children subject to the provisions of S.34 and those in accommodation.

'Even where birth families are marginalised by the care process, they remain an important source of continuity. The powerful psychological influence of the 'hidden' internalised parent has been known for many decades even if it is not always remembered and appreciated.' Now the Dartington researchers have pointed out that frequent changes of placement and social workers mean that the birth family may be in fact be the most stable influence in the child's experience even if actual contact is very limited' (Patterns and Outcomes in Child Placements.) Birth parents and the extended family by virtue of their very existence are a frame of reference which confirms and re-enforces the child's unique identity as a member of that family. In order to provide a similar frame of reference, substitute carers have to put in months and years of painstaking work.

Contact with Siblings

Scant attention has sometimes been paid to contact with siblings who have a crucial role to play in providing a sense of identity and activity for the child. Links with siblings should be jealously preserved and fostered, and guardians should not accept care plans which include the separation of siblings without good reason.

Support Services to Children and Families

Part III of the Act deals with local authority support for children and families and envisages that family support services will be offered to members of a family of a child in need, where the service is provided with a view to safeguarding and promoting the child's welfare. Local authority help for families may include:

* providing a home help or family aide;

* day care provision for a family member other than a child in need e.g. respite care.

In planning for the provision of services to children and family, local authorities will take account of the services offered by local voluntary organisations. Schedule 2 contains further provisions designed to promote the upbringing of children by their own families.

Participation in Decision Making

Parents, as well as children, should be given the opportunity to make their wishes and feelings known and to participate in decision making. They too have the right to make representation and complaints to the local authority under section 26 of the Act.

The Act allows parents greater opportunity to challenge local authority decision making by:

— diminishing the use of Wardship as a "back door into care";

— offering opportunities for parents to challenge decision making in the courts at an early stage; and

— eliminating internal administrative decision making procedures; for example, parental rights resolutions and procedures for terminating parental access to children in care.

Local authorities are required to:

— consult and inform parents at all stages;

— ascertain their wishes and feelings about placement plans;

— enter into written agreements, where possible;

— avoid compulsory measures as far as it is consistent with meeting children's needs;

— make arrangements for reasonable contact between parents or carers and children.

Parental Responsibility

The new concept of parental responsibility, (rather than rights) introduced by the Act, means that parents do not lose their parental responsibility for children who are subject to statutory orders. The only way to lose parental responsibility is through adoption. However, if a care order is made, the exercise of parental responsibility will be at the discretion of the local authority.

Parental responsibility includes the duty to provide financial support for children, so parents retain a financial responsibility for their children, even when they are in care. The financial responsibility is two-way however. The Children Act endorses the view that, in the majority of cases, it will be in the best interests of the children to grow up in their own biological family and places a duty on local authorities to provide the resources and services necessary to maintain children in their family home (see Part III of the Act). Guardians should bear in mind section 27 of the Act which facilitates co-operation between local health and education authorities and different local authority departments in providing appropriate services to children and families. Guardians will be in a position to test out the creative boundaries of section 27 and ensure, for example, that no child will come into care only because the parents are homeless.

Assessment of Parents

In making their assessment of the child's situation, guardians will need to look at the Department of Health Guide to Assessment and examine:

— the risk to the child within the family, i.e. risk of physical, sexual or emotional abuse or neglect.

— the capacity of the family to protect the child from an alleged abuser.

— the degree of responsibility accepted by the family for the child's current situation.

— evidence of the parents' determination, capacity and opportunity to change.

— the family's recognition of the need for help and willingness to co-operate with professionals in receiving such help.

— the degree of parents' warmth and affection towards the child and ability to put the needs of the child before their own.

— the availability of resources to provide the necessary services to children and families to ensure:

the protection necessary; and

the social work input that is both appropriate and adequate.

— what the parents have to offer the child, e.g. a strong sense of family identify and the security of 'belonging'—very easy for parents to bestow with comparatively little effort whereas it is much harder for substitute parents to re-create, especially in older children.

— whether the criteria for any orders are satisfied.

— evidence of parents working in partnership with the local authority.

— the way in which any agreements and contacts have been made or kept by parents (and the local authority).

— plans made for reasonable contact if the child is not living at home.

— the parents' capacity to stick to any agreed arrangements.

— what use parents have made of support services provided by the local authority under Part III of the Act, and what has been provided for them?

Foster Carers

The assumption of reasonable contact between children in care and their families has considerable implications for foster carers. Regulation 5 of the Arrangements for Placement of children (General) Regulations requires the local authority to enter into a written placement agreement with the foster carer. This will include a statement of the authority's plan for the child, information about the child and the arrangements being made to enable the child's parents to continue to play a part in the child's life. Guardians should check to see that the foster carers are clear about what is required of them both in relation to the child and his family.

Much is asked of foster carers in terms of flexibility and tolerance. Their attitude to the child's parents and extended family can have a profound influence on local authority planning and guardians should bear this in mind when assessing the suitability of particular foster parents to meet the long term needs of an individual child.

The assumption of reasonable contact will pose problems for some foster carers who, while happy to take on a child, may not be so happy to incorporate the child's parents as a regular feature in their lives and homes, particularly when they have children of their own to consider. Much depends on the clarity of the messages and expectations given to the foster carers by the placement worker. As long as the situation is made clear, then foster carers are able to make realistic judgements about what will be required. Things can go wrong if the expectations change after placement, to the distress of all concerned (see also Part IV, for the impact of the Children Act 1989 on fostering and adoption policies).

Residential Care and Carers

'The duty of public care is to deal with those children as if they were our own' Sir William Utting 'Children in Public Care — A Review of Residential Care' (HMSO 1991).

The purpose of residential care is to provide a home for children who:

* have decided that they do not wish to be fostered or adopted

* have had a bad experience of foster care

* have been so abused within the family that another family placement is inappropriate

* are from the same family and cannot otherwise be kept together

or who:

— need expert, multidisciplinary help with social and problems in a residential setting

— require containment and help in conditions of security (Utting: Conclusions and Recommendations).

Residential care has a key place in the range of options available to meet the needs of each individual child, and should be an integrated part of total child care provision. The spate of home closures in the 1980s meant that the numbers in residential care dropped by two thirds over 10 years to 13,200.

The 'Review of Residential Care' recommends local authorities consider urgently whether they are still able to provide a full range of services to children and young people. Clearly, the quality and stability of residential care available will have a bearing on the decision making in relation to children, and is something which should be borne in mind by guardians.

Volume 4 of the Regulations and Guidance deals with Residential Care. It also contains the Children's Homes Regulations 1991 and the Arrangements for Placement of Children (General) Regulations 1991. Guardians should be familiar with *all* these regulations which provide a framework for the public care of children. Paragraph 1.91 deals with matters of control and discipline and prohibits (except in certain prescribed circumstances)—

* any form of corporal punishment

* any deprivation of food and drink

* any restriction on visits to or by the child or any restriction on, or delay in communications by telephone or post with—his parent, relatives, social worker, solicitor and guardian ad litem, among others.

Residential care staff are themselves a disadvantaged group. Only 20% of them have recognized child care qualifications and they are one of the lowest paid groups in the personal social services workforce. Staff work long hours in stressful situations and guardians should be sensitive to the demanding nature of the job, and to the commitment of many staff to the children in their care. The quality of staff recruited is of prime importance:-

> 'Children in residential care are vulnerable to exploitation by adults and to both physical and sexual abuse. Employers should offer protection in these areas by carefully scrutinizing and where necessary, investigating the credentials and antecedents of staff and others, such as visitors and volunteers who come into close contact with children in care'. (Utting, paragraph 24).

Sadly children are abused in care just as they are abused in their own homes. Until recently however the abuse has not attracted the same attention or the same credibility as abuse by parents and foster carers. It is painful for professionals to acknowledge that abuse occurs in care,and it is often harder to listen to children in residential care, as it involves being prepared to believe that social work staff may have been involved in the abuse. Guardians should be particularly vigilant in looking at the position of children in residential care as they are exceptionally vulnerable.

The events which led to the Staffordshire 'Pin-down' and the Leicestershire child abuse inquiry clearly illustrate the need for an independent outside opinion when decisions are being made about children in public care.

Chapter 9

Working with Local Authorities

A major part of the guardian ad litem's role in relation to the local authority is to provide for the court a critical appraisal of the local authority's policy, practice and planning in relation to the particular child or children. In this context guardians will find it helpful to refer to:

— Volumes 2 (Family Support, Day Care and Educational Provision for Young Children), 3 (Family Placement) and 4 (Residential Care) of the Children Act Guidance and Regulations;

— "The Care of children—Principles and Practice in Regulations and Guidance", HMSO 1989;

— "Child Care Policy—Putting it in writing", HMSO 1990;

— "Children in Need and their Families—A new approach (A Guide to Part III of the Children Act 1989 for local authority councillors), University of Leicester and Department of Health 1990.

Services to Children and Families

Under the Children Act 1989, local authorities have a duty to seek to maintain children in their family home (Schedule 2) and to provide a range and level of services appropriate to the children in need in their area. Guardians should note that because the definition of 'children in need' is in the Act, a local authority cannot lawfully substitute any other definition for the purposes of fulfilling their responsibilities under Part III—providing services to children and families. The definition of "need" in section 17 of the Act is deliberately made to emphasise the importance of preventative support and services to families. Children in need are those:

* unlikely to achieve or maintain or have the opportunity of achieving or maintaining a reasonable standard of health or development without the provision of services;

* those whose health or development is likely to be significantly impaired or further impaired without the provision of such services;

* those who are disabled.

The following provisions deal with some essential local authority duties under the Act:

Section 22 sets out the general duty of local authorities in relation to children looked after by them (this section replaces section 18 of the Child Care Act 1980).

Section 22(3)

> *"It shall be the duty of a local authority looking after any child:*
>
> *(a)   to safeguard and promote his welfare; and*
>
> *(b)   to make such use of services available for children cared for by their own parents as appears to the authority reasonable in his case".*

Section 22(4)

"Before making any decision with respect to a child whom they are looking after, or proposing to look after, a local authority shall, so far as is reasonably practicable, ascertain the wishes and feelings of—

(a)   the child;

(b)   his parents;

(c)   any other person who is not a parent of his but who has parental responsibility for him; and

(d)   any other person whose wishes and feelings the authority consider to be relevant, regarding the matter to be decided".

Section 22(5)

"In making any such decision a local authority shall give due consideration:

(a)   having regard to his age and understanding, to such wishes and feelings of the child as they have been able to ascertain;

(b)   to such wishes and feelings of any person mentioned in subsections 4(b) to (d) as they have been able to ascertain; and

(c)   to the child's religious persuasion, racial origin, cultural and linguistic background."

The guardian ad litem should:

— ascertain the stated policy, procedures and practice of the local authority;

— examine how those policies, procedures and practices are working out in reality and in planning for the future of this particular child (particular attention should be paid to the existence of any "blanket" policies which, although illegal under the Act, may be still skewing the planning in relation to an individual child;

"All factors relevant to the welfare of the individual child must be taken into account in assessing the child's needs and making decisions about the child's welfare. None of the separate factors involved should be abstracted and converted into a general precondition which over-rides the others or causes any of them to be less than fully considered. The only general policy that is acceptable in making decisions about placing children is that all relevant factors should be considered. Different factors will obviously vary in importance in relation to different children or in relation to the same child at different times. It will be right in those circumstances to weigh different factors differently. But it is not right to define any factor as of such general significance or primacy that it over-rides or qualifies the duty to consider together all factors bearing on the welfare of the child as an individual". (Para 2.22. of Volumes 3 or 4 of the Children Act Regulations and Guidance.)

— examine the local authority file in order to:

  *   establish an accurate and chronological view of events;

  *   check for factual inaccuracies and confusions of act and opinion. In particular check that hearsay evidence has not acquired the status of truth through frequent repetition:

  *   examine how the process of decision making has evolved; and

*   check the appropriateness of the local authority plan in the context of the evidence.

*   advise the court as to whether the order sought by the local authority is appropriate and suggest alternatives where necessary. (However, if guardians recommend a section 8 order rather than a care order they should bear in mind that the local authority *cannot be compelled* to provide the resources to make the order work, or be forced to work in certain directions).

Attendance of Parents/Carers and Children at all Reviews and Case Conferences

Chapter 8 of the Children Act 1989 Guidance and Regulations Volume 3—and Chapter 3 of Volume 4, deal with reviews of children's cases. See also the Children and Young Persons (Review of Children's Cases) Regulations 1991 (Statutory Instrument No. 895), and the revised "Working Together" (1991).

Regulation 7(2) of the Review of Children's Cases Regulations requires that the responsible authority, where they consider it appropriate, should involve the child and his parents in review meetings. The possibility of a child being accompanied by friendly support should be considered. In addition to the parents and child, the child's carers should also be invited and any other person with a legitimate interest in the child who has a contribution to make. This may apply, for example, to the child's GP, the community health doctor, health visitor, child psychologist, teacher, foster parent, residential care social worker, independent visitor (if appointed), ethnic minority representative or interpreter. The attendance of such people should always be discussed with the child before invitations are made as he may have a view about their attendance.

Health Reviews

The responsible authority has a duty to make arrangements for a child in care or provided with accommodation by them to be examined by a registered medical practitioner and for a written assessment on the state of health of the child and his need for health care to be made:

"(a)   at least once in every period of six months before the child's second birthday; and

(b)   at least once in every period of twelve months after the child's second birthday unless the child is of sufficient understanding and he refuses to submit to the examination." (Regulation 6).

Reviews are also held under the provisions of the 1981 Education Act for children with special needs.

Practical aspects of 'care' are often overlooked so that children in care may be receiving sophisticated psychotherapeutic support but may have rotting teeth or ill-fitting shoes. Guardians should check that the health reviews have been carried out and that children have had, for example, regular visits to the dentist, optician and orthodontist if necessary. These omissions very often occur because the local authority is a "fragmented parent" and functions in relation to the child are divided. The guardian may be the only person who is in a position to take a holistic view of the child's life and functioning and the guardian's subsequent report will be a valuable resource which may inform decision making in the future. Health considerations to which responsible authorities are to have regard are listed in Regulation 7 and Schedule 2 of the (Arrangements for Placement of Children (General) Regulations 1991 (Statutory Instrument No 890) and in Schedule 3 of the Review of Children's Cases Regulations 1991 (Statutory Instrument No 895). They include the requirement to have regard to "the possible need for an appropriate course of action which should be identified to assist necessary change of such care, treatment or surveillance."

Case Conferences and Key Planning Meetings

Guardians should always avoid becoming part of the collective decision making process inherent in case conference procedures. However, if there is a specific reason for the guardian to attend, or the court directs that the guardian should do so, then clearly the situation must be regarded flexibly. A specific exception to this rule may be in the attendance at a case conference following an application for an emergency protection order, when all professionals concerned are working to a very tight timetable. There may be two reasons for the guardian to attend such a case conference:

— to facilitate matters through a swift exchange of information at the case conference;

— to ensure an adequate representation of the child's wishes and feelings in relation to the application.

"Working Together", stresses the importance of both parents and children being encouraged to attend case conferences. Part 6 deals with the Child Protection Conference and the Child Protection Register and recommends that both parents and children are encouraged to attend case conferences. If the parent's solicitor is present it may be that the child's solicitor and guardian should also be present. The child too, of course, if of an age and understanding, should be given the opportunity to attend. This would also apply to the guardian's attendance at child protection reviews.

It is helpful also if the guardian requests the person taking the minutes to note that they are there, not as part of the decision making process, but for a specific purpose which may be stated in the record. Guardians should request a copy of the agenda and minutes of the meeting.

As well as looking at factors specific to individual children, guardians ad litem will be looking at the general policies and practices of the local authority concerned. The Department of Health Document "Child Abuse—A Study of Inquiry Reports 1980-1989" (HMSO 1991) and the earlier study of Inquiry Reports 1973-1981 are particularly useful in highlighting areas in which local authority planning for children can go disastrously wrong.

Organisational problems

High turnover of staff can have a profound effect on relationships and communication between agencies. Unfilled vacancies, inexperience among newly promoted managers and longer serving ones at the end of their tether can lead to a siege mentality (Doreen Aston Inquiry, paragraph 5.17).

Staff shortages and shortage of black workers

Despite the fact that seven of the Inquiries relate to black and ethnic minority children, issues relating to the recruitment of black staff are barely touched upon ("Child Abuse—A Study of Inquiry Reports 1980-1989", page 37).

Miscellaneous problems

Lack of adequate cover for social workers during leave and sickness can produce major problems. It is often the case that there is very little leeway in the system to provide adequate cover for absences due to sickness, leave or people on training courses.

Unallocated cases

A substantial number of Inquiries refer to inadequate administrative and clerical support and the absence of adequate departmental administrative procedures.

Lack of resources

The Inquiries note the poverty of physical resources in social services departments. Some of the buildings available are not suitable for the carrying out of delicate and sensitive interviews. In addition these may be shortages of:

— Background resources—the physical environment e.g. housing and education.

— The resources aimed at the case. The Tyra Henry Inquiry drew attention to the unforgivable decline in human and material resources which formed not only the backdrop to, but a main precipitant of, Tyra's tragedy. "Its remedy lies in more powerful hands than Lambeth's" (Tyra Henry Inquiry paragraph 8.21).

The Kimberley Carlisle Inquiry (Paragraph 78) concluded "It is the responsibility of senior management, local and central government to provide the overall resources and to determine the broad pattern of priorities for these resources, taking responsibility for decisions leading to no or limited services being provided."

The "A" inquiry recommended that the County Council take note of the major resource implications which would result from the Children Act 1989 and ensure that, in the light of these implications, it is able to fulfil its statutory duties in relation to child protection ("A" Inquiry paragraph 13).

Levels of skills

The Doreen Aston Inquiry in 1989 stated that it was normal practice within the authority for professionally qualified social workers to be allocated child abuse cases within a few months of starting work and if this could not continue to be the case it was highly likely that a significant number of child abuse cases would be unallocated (CCETSW Research showed that 25% of newly qualified social workers were working on child abuse cases within one year of qualification).

Training

The Tyra Henry Inquiry addressed a particular training issue. "The problem of 'positive' racial stereotypes needs to be fully addressed both in the training of social workers (and associated professionals too) and in a more considered deployment of black social workers to work with black families. We are not thinking of racial matching or anything like it in making the latter part of this recommendation. We are concerned to ensure, where there is doubt or difficulty about the cultural aspects of behaviour or lifestyle, the input and evaluation of a social worker of similar background." (Tyra Henry Inquiry page 109).

Guardians should always bear in mind that the level of state intervention into family life (particularly of the poor) varies:-

> 'Since the mid 1970s the purpose of state intervention has been shifting. It has been much more significantly concerned with monitoring family life, and stepping into protect vulnerable individuals from cruel or neglectful families. The notion of support or supplementation of family care has weakened, as the social services have come to be seen as expensive, and a potential drain on national prosperity. But the need for more controlling measures by the state in the family's sphere of influence has been increasingly emphasised.' Bill Jordan Invitation to Social Work (1984).

The Children Act 1989 seeks to redress this imbalance by emphasising the responsibilities of local authorities to provide support services to children and families. The task of the guardian in relation to local authorities is to act as a balancing agent in this complex equation. In carrying out their duties, guardians should be aware of the social and economic climate in which local authorities operate, and also be aware of how general factors which have little to do with the behaviour of individual families, affect and control the local authority response.

If the resources are not available to meet the needs of a particular family guardians should state this unequivocally so that a clear picture of how the Act is being implemented will emerge, in a way that can only be helpful to children and families and to local authority colleagues.

"Working Together"—police and social workers

Social workers have a statutory duty to protect the child in those circumstances and are therefore not only entitled to proceed in cases where the police feel unable to act, but have a duty to the child to do so. This duty may not always be fully appreciated by the police. It is therefore important for guardians to look at the working relationships between the police and the social services department with particular care (see "Working Together", HMSO 1991. Part 4 The Police).

Extension of the guardian's role in relation to local authorities

The Children Act 1989 imposes great responsibilities on local authorities, both in the provision of services and in the allocation of resources to pay for them. By giving guardians a new case management role under the Court Rules, panel members will be required to:

— scrutinise and comment on local authorities' evidence and applications;

— intervene at an earlier stage in the proceedings;

— advise the court whether the order sought or any other is appropriate; and

— monitor the local authority's efforts to:

  * maintain the child in his family home;

  * work in partnership with parents;

  * facilitate reasonable contact between parent and child.

This is a role which must be handled sensitively by panel members. Gratuitous criticism is never welcome. Critical appraisal of the local authority's work must be both objective and of direct relevance to the case. If there are any general practice and policy issues which may inform future local authority practice, these should be fed back to the local authority by means of a letter to the Director and to the Family Court Business Committee after the termination of the case.

Guardians are often loathe to criticise colleagues in social services departments who may be extremely hard pressed and demoralised. Accepting or colluding with things that are wrong within the system, is, however, not a constructive way of helping to improve matters for either children or social workers. Guardians' reports will now be subjected to much more effective systems of central collation and monitoring which will include the production of an annual panel report. They therefore provide a bird's eye view of local authorities' practices and policies and will be a valuable source of statistical evidence about how the Act is being implemented and what improvements may be required. In this way guardians will inform as well as critically appraise practice.

Chapter 10

Working with the Court and the Child's Solicitor

WORKING WITH THE COURT

Allocation of Proceedings

Most public law applications will start in the local Family Proceedings Court. However, in certain circumstances cases can be transferred to a higher court or another Family Proceedings court. The circumstances are prescribed in Article 7(1) of the Children (Allocation of Proceedings) Order 1991 (Statutory Instrument No. 1677). See Guidance and Regulations Volume 7 Annex I. For example, the grounds for transfer from a magistrates' court to a county court care centre of public law cases are:

(a) where the proceedings are exceptionally grave, important or complex;

(b) where it would be appropriate for the proceedings to be heard together with other family proceedings which are pending in another court; or

(c) where transfer is likely significantly to accelerate the determination of the proceedings and where delay would seriously prejudice the child's interests.

Guardians should be aware that one of the key principle in determining case allocation is that delay is likely to prejudice the welfare of the child and must be avoided in all cases, except where it can be clearly demonstrated that the delay will be of some constructive benefit to the child. Delays for judicial or administrative convenience are no longer acceptable.

In appointing a solicitor for the child, guardians should be satisfied that they will have sufficient time available to spend on the case within the required time table.

Legal Aid

Solicitors are required to apply to the Legal Aid Board in writing. In urgent cases, applications may be made by telephone and a decision given the same day. Guardians may refer to The Legal Aid Regulations. See Guidance and Regulations Volume 7 Annex K.

Working with the Court

The family proceedings court and the clerk will be looking to the guardian to provide information to assist in determining the appropriate allocation and timetabling of the case as well as giving advice as to the appropriateness or otherwise of the order(s) sought.

Parent's application to discharge an emergency protection order after seventy-two hours

The timetable for an emergency protection order is very tight and the guardian needs to move into action quickly. It is anticipated that one of the directions given on the granting of an emergency protection order will be for the appointment of a guardian. The guardian may have only limited information to make available to the court at a hearing for the discharge of an emergency protection order, but should make every effort to marshal as much information as possible for the court, e.g., as to the continuing need for the child to be kept away from home, the availability of a suitable carer from the extended family, etc.

The first directions appointment or hearing

The directions or (order(s)) made by the court at the first hearing are likely to set the pattern for later decisions and are therefore crucial. The court will need to be as fully apprised as possible of the situation of the child and the family in order to make the appropriate decision. That information will come from various sources, e.g.., the local authority, the parents and their legal representatives, but again the guardian will have a key role in gathering and assessing information for the court. The court will also need information to help it make decisions about *allocation* and *timetabling*.

Allocation of proceedings

It is essential that the decision on the allocation of proceedings should be taken as soon as possible, in order not to delay the progress of the case. It is also essential that it be the appropriate decision based on the fullest information available, so that more time is not lost by a need to reconsider that decision at a later stage if, for example, further relevant information comes to light;

Timetabling

The guardian is in a key position to see all the parties and gather information about a number of issues:

* the time within which assessments can be made and reports prepared;

* those persons whom it is appropriate for the court to join as parties;

* things that are not being done, e.g.., orders not being complied with.

The guardian should be prepared to supply this information at various stages of the proceedings:

* at a hearing before the full court;

* at a directions hearing before a single justice or a clerk;

* at any time that the information becomes available.

This latter point is particularly important. Precious time is lost if information about the development of the case is known but not shared.

Appropriate channels for providing the court with this information will depend on local practice but however it is done it is *essential* that guardians take account of their role as the gatherer and sharer of relevant information about the case.

The court will now, more than ever, be looking to the guardian as *the voice of the child*, given the emphasis in the Children Act on the child's views and wishes being ascertained and taken into account. The court will also seek guidance on the appropriateness of the order(s) being sought, on whether a different "package" would suit this particular child and, of course, on whether any order should be made at all.

The guardian will always bear in mind the basic principles of the Act, that unnecessary delay is deleterious to the child, that orders should only be made if they are likely to be of positive benefit to the child, and that the voice of the child should always be heard. Those are the principles that will guide the guardian in her dealings with the child and with the court.

WORKING WITH THE CHILD'S SOLICITOR

The guardian's new case management role and much closer relationship with the courts should not be allowed to undermine the establishment of a working partnership between the guardian and child care law solicitor, so essential to the effective representation of children. The child's solicitor will continue to be the guardian's main source of consultation and support during the investigation.

Party Status and Legal Representation

Children will be full parties in all public proceedings under the Children Act 1989. The guardian must ensure that the child is indeed a party and appoint a suitable solicitor, bearing in mind the facts of the case and the child involved.

Guardians are encouraged to select a solicitor from the local panel of child care solicitors, although this is not compulsory. Solicitors on the list will vary considerably in their experience and expertise of child care law and practice and should be chosen with care, according to the needs of each case. Guardians should be wary of a solicitor who is not keen to meet the child, even if the child is only a few months old. Seeing the child will serve to bring him alive in the mind of his legal representative and help to focus his representation of the child's interests in court.

To some extent it is a case of "horses for courses". If the case involves allegations of sexual abuse a solicitor with experience of dealing with such cases should be instructed if possible. Other factors to take into consideration are advocacy skills, especially if the case is to be fiercely contested and the travelling distances between the solicitor, child, guardian ad litem and the court. A solicitor is appointed to the child care law panel on the understanding that he or she will undertake the cases personally and not send their articled clerk if it happens to be an inconvenient day. The Court Rules (Rule 12(4)) provide for guardians to apply to court to change the solicitor if they feel unhappy, so they are in a strong position to require a competent level of representation for the child. Obviously, if the solicitor is ill or a conflict of interest arises the solicitor may have to be changed. This may apply equally to the guardian. Just as the courts should avoid always appointing the same guardian and thus risking the development of collusive relationships, so too guardians should appoint as wide a range of solicitors as practicable. In practice solicitors and guardians have been working together very constructively and there is every reason to think this will continue.

Apportioning the Work

Once a solicitor has been appointed, the guardian should arrange a meeting as soon as possible to discuss:

— allocation of work; who will see which witnesses; should interviews be carried out alone or together and where they should take place;

— allocation of the case —which court is appropriate;

— timetabling—the onus will now be on all concerned to keep delay to a minimum;

— obtaining any relevant documentation e.g. details of criminal records or previous hearings;

— listing possible witnesses or expert witnesses and making sure that the solicitor goes through their evidence with them;

— receiving and acting on relevant documents received on behalf of the child. If documents from the local authority file are to be produced in evidence under the provisions contained in section 42, the child's solicitor should notify the local authority's legal department of the evidence to be adduced.

— planning the introduction of the solicitor to his client—the child, and deciding where and when this should take place;

Analysing the Available Information and Planning the Presentation of the Case in Court

Once the guardian and solicitor have completed the bulk of the investigation they will:-

— discuss the guardian's recommendation on the basis of the available information, including any expert witnesses evidence;

— discuss the available orders and options and arrangements for contact;

— take a view on the child's ability to give separate instructions if these conflict with those of the guardian;

— consider the child's attendance at court, taking into account the child's age, understanding and stated wishes;

— consider the child's ability to make an informed decision regarding consent to medical or other examination;

— plan the presentation of the child's case, making sure an interpreter is available if necessary;

— review the list of witnesses and add any necessary;

— study the reports and statements from all other parties and identify areas of contentious evidence;

— scrutinise the local authority case and the needs of the child in relation to the order sought.

Two Weeks before the Hearing

— go through the guardian's report together and with the child—depending on the child's age and capacity to understand. Wherever possible the child should understand what is being proposed on his behalf.

Ten Days before the Hearing

— lodge the report with the court. The Court Rules require that the guardian ad litem shall *"unless the justices' clerk or the court otherwise directs, not less than 7 days before the date fixed for the final hearing of the proceedings, file a written report advising on the interests of the child"* (Rule 11(7)). Good practice would dictate that panel members should aim to lodge reports ten days before the hearing, in order to ensure that the court has time to copy reports and circulate them to the relevant parties. Guardians should note that, although all reports and documentation relating to the case will be discussed in advance of the hearing, it may be in certain sensitive situations not all the evidence should be disclosed to all. If this is the case the guardian should inform the court at the time the report is lodged taking care to identify the information concerned;

— check with the court that the report has been circulated to the other parties in good time to avoid any unnecessary adjournment;

— prepare the final details of the child's case; make sure witnesses have been notified of the time and place of hearing and they have the means and directions to get there;

— if the child is attending the court: familiarise him with the surroundings and explain how he will get there, who else will be there and how the proceedings will be conducted;

— check the waiting room arrangements and court facilities, in case there are people the child would rather not see, (for example, if an abusing parent is present) and make sure there will be a suitable room to see people alone if necessary;

— consider the likelihood of an appeal becoming necessary.

On the Day of the Hearing

— attend the court with the child's solicitor, arriving at least one hour before the hearing to avoid last minute hitches and confusion;

— check with the child's solicitor that the witnesses have arrived;

— reassure and support the child (if present) through the court waiting time;

— sit next to the child (if that is what he wants) and the solicitor in court in order to help in the management and progress of the case, e.g. indicating a new area of questioning, or alerting the solicitor to contradictory or inaccurate information.

After the Hearing:

— make sure that the child understands the outcome and the decision made, or explain how long it will be necessary to wait until the bench give their decisions and the reasons;

— 'de-brief' with the solicitor—discuss whether or not any other action is necessary i.e.

  * appeal (within 21 days) on behalf of the child;

  * any eligibility under the Criminal Injuries Compensation Scheme for the child to claim compensation for: pain, suffering or shock arising out of acts of rape and sexual offences, or any other type of abuse or attack.

— make sure the other parties understand what the court has decided. Although strictly not the role of the guardian or the child's solicitor to do this, it is often the case that it is left to them to explain to parents what has happened. Now that the courts have to give reasons for their decisions, parents should not be left in a state of confusion;

— lodge an appeal within twenty one days, if appropriate.

— made sure that the child knows of the existence and purpose of the representations and complaints procedure (S.26).

PART III

THE ISSUES

Chapter 11

The Role of the Guardian ad Litem

INDEPENDENCE

Crucial to the panel member's role is functioning as an independent professional.

> "The right of children to separate and independent representation in public law hearings is a central tenet of the Children Act. It is essential that GALROs, in reaching their judgements about the welfare of each child, should 'continue to be independent of the local authority or other organisation providing the service. Arrangements for the management of the panel and the day to day work of the GALRO must take full account of this requirement within the existing legal framework of ultimate accountability residing with the local authority." (Children Act Guidance and Regulations Volume 7 paragraph 2.4)

Panels have been created, not just because of the need for another voice in children's proceedings, but for an *independent* voice to assess the evidence and act as a representative for children in the courts. It is the independence of that representation which is of critical importance and which, by providing a different perception of the case, acts as a safeguard for the child. Independence therefore is important, not just as a concept, but as a safety net at a crossroads in the child's life. Independence must be maintained, not just to the satisfaction of the local authorities, but to the satisfaction of the child, the other parties, the judiciary and the public at large. Guardians are accountable to the courts, and must assure them that their independence from other parties to the proceedings is not compromised.

There are four separate aspects of independence:

— Independence of professional opinion;

— Personal independence;

— Perceived independence;

— An administratively independent structure from which to operate.

Independence of Professional Opinion

If the guardians ad litem are to be effective in performing their duty to *safeguard the welfare of the child*, it is essential that they act and are seen to act independently of the employing authority or agency (if they have one) and of the authority administering the panel. When acting as guardians ad litem, their work in relation to the child is not subject to the professional scrutiny and direction of the panel manager. This applies to all panel members, including probation officers. Constraint is often, by its very nature, invisible. If panel members feel that they are being subjected to constraints on their independence they should declare these to the court, to the Panel Manager and Panel Committee. It is worth remembering that if constraints on independence are not declared then they will be assumed not to exist.

Guardians ad litem are unique amongst social services personnel in that they are personally accountable to the courts for the work they carry out. They are not part of a line management structure, and the decisions they make are autonomous rather than arrived at as part of a collective decision-making process. Their role has developed from both a legal and social work background as an independent expert witness, and it is in that capacity that they appear before the court. They must therefore be credible as being both 'independent' and 'expert' in general (not specialist) child care matters. There can, however, be no power without responsibility. The problem in relation to guardians is how to combine the proper degree of professional accountability with the necessary amount of professional independence. This has to be achieved without undermining the ability of the service to fulfil its proper function—that of safeguarding the interests of the child.

Research findings (Higginson 1990 and DHSS 1982) have endorsed the view that one huge drawback of the bureaucratic collective decision-making process is its apparent inability to change course in the face of new evidence. Instead, evidence is sought to reinforce decisions already made.

The value of an experienced, skilled, and independent opinion in this context should not be under-estimated. Research, procedures and guidelines can assist good practice but they are no substitute for it. The skill of an experienced practitioner exercising her independent, professional judgement in relation to the needs of an individual child in a particular situation is invaluable.

Personal Independence

There may, exceptionally, be times when guardians ad litem feel that they cannot offer an objective view about a case because of some raw or unresolved experience in their own lives. If this is the case then it should be stated at the outset so that the work can be undertaken by another panel member. It is in relation to matters of personal conflict of interest that support and consultation with colleagues (within the bounds of confidentiality) can be particularly valuable. However, there will be situations in which the guardian will feel the need for individual consultation and this should also be available (see Children Act Guidance and Regulations, Volume 7, para 2.22).

The question of personal eligibility also has a bearing on personal independence. The Court Rules (Rule 10(7)) stipulate that a panel member should not have been concerned with a particular child in the 5 years before their appointment to the Panel. The guidance accompanying the GALRO (Panels) Regulations (Volume 7, Chapter 2), however, makes it clear that guardians should be their own watchdogs in this matter. It may be that the GALRO's direct concern with the family dates back further than five years, and in such circumstances it is strongly recommended that the GALRO advises the court that an alternative appointment should be made.

> "Where Panels have consortia or reciprocal arrangements the possibility of a GALRO employed by a local authority having knowledge of a particular case will be reduced but not removed. It will also be easier for alternative GALROs to be found. Single authority Panels will need to ensure that flexibility to provide suitable GALROs is not restricted by drawing a large proportion of their membership from the category of employee of the local authority, particularly if those persons formerly were employed as social workers with a child care remit in that local authority." (Paragraph 2.48, Volume 7)

Perceived Independence

In the interests of natural justice it is important that the guardian is, and is seen to be, independent by all other parties. This means maintaining true independence, not just to the satisfaction of the administering local authority, but also to the satisfaction of all other parties to the proceedings, the judiciary and the general public. If the service is not perceived to be independent its credibility will be undermined and devalued in a way which would be detrimental to the interests of children.

Perceived independence is not just a superficial concept—a service will not be perceived to be independent unless it is based on administrative structures which have accepted and incorporated the need for independence into all service arrangements.

Administrative Independence

The debate about any possible the conflict of interest inherent in local authorities (who are one party to the proceedings) administering and funding a safety net service for children (another party to the proceedings) has been an area of contention since the establishment of the panels in 1984. The question of the GALRO service becoming part of a wider support service for the family jurisdiction is the subject of the Lord Chancellor's rolling programme of reform. There may in the future be more fundamental changes. However, for the time being Panels will continue to be administered and funded by local authorities. Local authorities should ensure the independence of the panels in accordance with the regulations.

The Children Act Guidance and Regulations, Volume 7, Chapter 2 sets out a number of requirements to secure the independence of the Panels:

— the employment of a panel manager who is at 'arms length' from the administering local authority, and who carries no other responsibilities for that local authority's child care policies and practices;

— the setting up of a panel committee with an independent chair and membership;

— arranging (but not personally providing) appropriate training, consultation and support;

— the provision of a direct telephone line, separate postal address and appropriately printed notepaper for panels.

Role of the panel manager

The role of the panel manager is to facilitate the efficient and professional operation of the Panel in order to provide an effective service to children involved in public law proceedings. To that end panel managers will be concerned with the deployment of the guardians, rather than supplying professional advice in respect of individual cases. A list of the panel manager's responsibilities is set out in Volume 7 at paragraph 2.23.

"GALROs need to judge the extent of enquiries necessary in each individual case to which they are appointed. If there is uncertainty as to whether in a particular case the work proposed by the GALRO is appropriate and necessary, then the proper channel for this to be clarified is likely to be through the directions hearings under the provisions of the Court Rules (Rules 14 and 11(4)(f), or equivalent advice and direction from the court dealing with the adoption proceedings." (Volume 7 para 2.37)

It is not lawful for a local authority to seek to impose a limit on the number of hours a guardian may spend on a particular case. The High Court in a judgment in November 1991 following a Judicial Review commended the advice in Volume 7 and warned local authorities against imposing blanket limitations on work which the guardian might consider to be necessary. In conclusion Sir Stephen Brown said:

'I wish to emphasise how vital it is for guardians not only to be seen to be independent but also to be able to be assured themselves of their independence in the carrying out of their duties.' (Judicial Review Cornwall and Isles of Scilly Panel of Guardians and Litem and Reporting Officers and Cornwall Social Services Department Nov 5th 1991.)

Complaints

The procedures to be followed in the event of a complaint against a Panel member are set out in the Guidance and Regulations, Volume 7, Chapter 2.

Each Panel shall establish a procedure for dealing with complaints, and a Complaints Board whose members are independent of the local authority which established the Panel in the event of a continuing dispute (which may include the question of non-reappointment to the Panel). There is no stipulation of a time limit for the resolution of complaints. It is likely to be in everyone's' interest to resolve any matter within three months of the complaint being formally lodged, otherwise the guardian may be placed in an invidious position professionally, and the Panel may be deprived of one of its members for an unjustifiably long period.

Reviews

The enhancement of the guardian's independence does not mean that they should be cut off from appropriate professional feedback and review, and guardians very much welcome this process as a way of improving practice. The GALRO (Panels) Regulations and associated guidance require a review of the guardian's work in the first year following appointment. A further review is required in the first year following reappointment.

Training, consultation and support

The guidance requires basic categories of training; such as:

— induction training;

— development and updating training;

— specialist training (i.e., children with special needs);

In addition, guardians should liaise with panel managers and other panel members about the provision of individual consultation and group support.

Fees

It is a matter for each local authority to fix its own rates. However, it will be counter productive for the discrepancy between rates in different areas to be excessively wide as this will distort the pattern of availability of guardians in certain areas, and will lead to delays. The Law Society rate for independent reporting is reviewed annually in April, and is widely accepted as a fair baseline from which to calculate fees.

CHILD'S REPRESENTATIVE OR COURT OFFICER?

Is the Role Child-led or Court-centred?

The new case management role for guardians introduced under section 41(10) of the Act presupposes that they will in future be working much more closely with courts and with court officials. This should not however detract from their central role as independent representatives of children. The purpose of their liaison and communication with the court is not to ease the passage of the case through the courts as an end in itself but to secure the welfare of the child by so doing. Guardians, court officials and members of the judiciary will have to test out the boundaries of the new roles and it is very important that following implementation of the

Act, guardians emphasise the child as their central concern. The unified jurisdiction is new. They should be aware that the court structure may present problems and should be prepared to comment on any shortcomings or failures in communication, both in their reports and as part of their new general and regular feed back to the designated judge and the Family Court Service Committee. Panel members should not be afraid of using the substantial new powers which they are being given nor of exploring the boundaries of their role in relation to courts on behalf of the children they represent. In the same way as the new provisions in 1984 introduced the concept of a working partnership between guardians and solicitors, so the Children Act 1989 introduces the concept of partnership between guardians and justices clerks.

The purpose of the partnership is to:

— avoid delays;

— allocate cases to the appropriate court;

— make sure that appropriate hearings for directions and cases are efficiently timetabled and arranged.

One of the drawbacks of the previous legislation was the lack of guardians' direct liaison with the justices' clerks and the judiciary and there are opportunities in the new arrangements to forge effective links with the courts and to expedite children's proceedings.

The key word here is partnership. Guardians feared in 1984 that they would become errand runners for solicitors. This proved not to be the case and guardians and solicitors work together in mutual respect. The same should be true of guardians' new relationship with justices' clerks.

Boundaries of the Role

The powers and responsibilities of the guardian ad litem are now quite awesome in their scope. Previous discussions about whether or not guardians should seek to promote change are now academic, as guardians have an extensive remit under section 41(10) and the court rules to advise the court in virtually every aspect of every case.

In particular, guardians will have the opportunity to recommend that proceedings be diverted away from Part IV and V of the Act to Part III—support for children and families. In this way, guardians will have a powerful impact on how the Act is implemented, and the level at which the state intervenes in family life. They should, however, carry out their duties with the awareness that it is the local authority social worker who has the day to day responsibility for the child and who is responsible for any ongoing decision making. For example, a guardian may wish to arrange a contact visit between parent and child if this has not been done in order to assess the interaction between them. This should only be done in consultation with the local authority social worker who is responsible for the case.

Naturally guardians cannot continue to be involved with a child until they achieve adulthood. However, the guardian's recommendation should take account of the adult the child will become and recommend a course of action which will not be limited to the short term interests of babyhood or adolescence but will fulfil any potential the child possesses. It will not be the case that guardians will need to use all their powers in all cases. One of the skills will be in deciding the extent of the duties in a particular case. The involvement of the guardian may be wide-ranging and extend over a considerable number of weeks—equally it may be limited to one particular and fairly specific function. For example, under the specified proceedings;

— advising the court about the advisability of allowing a change of surname; or

— the removal of the child from the United Kingdom.

The Act gives guardians the power and discretion to carry out their duties in a variety of different ways. Indeed, the court in certain cases may specifically request that the guardian focus their enquiries only on a specific number of issues.

Resources

Guardians are aware that in some cases the resources necessary to meet the needs of the child are not available in the area. If this is the case, a two tier recommendation could be considered. The first, a statement of what is necessary to meet the needs of this particular child and the second, a more pragmatic recommendation on the basis of making the best use of the resources available. In this way courts, the Family Court Business Committee and the local authority may be aware of the resources being made available to meet the needs of children in their area.

Panel Membership and Anti-discriminatory Practice

It is a source of regret and a weakness of current panel membership that there are so few guardians from ethnic minority groups. Panels should aim at a membership which reflects the ethnic balance of the communities they serve; this will not be achieved without positive policies of recruitment and training.

Violence

Guardians often work in more isolation than local authority colleagues. They should take care to let somebody reliable know where they are and what time they expect to return. Guardians should talk to panel managers about arrangements to be accompanied in situations of potential violence and investigate the possibility of providing electrical pocket alarm systems, and making available 'neutral ground' on which to carry out interviews. Guardians may like to refer to the British Association of Social Workers document "Violence to Social Workers".

Staff Care

Many panel members are in a situation of operational and professional isolation. The mental and physical demands of the role—always onerous, have now increased dramatically. Guardians should not under-estimate the wear and tear of the job and administering authorities should be encouraged to build in mechanisms to:-

— ensure the safety of guardians by making sure that sufficient back-up is available to support them in vulnerable or potentially violent situations;

— ensure that guardians are encouraged and enabled to "de-brief " after prolonged court hearings or traumatic visits;

— provide facilities for panel members to meet to exchange information and provide mutual support;

— recognise that it is not advisable to work at the same rate year after year without a change of pace or area of involvement.

Recognising that you need support is not a sign of weakness—it is a realistic recognition of the strains inherent in the job.

Code of Ethics

The National Association of Guardians ad Litem and Reporting Officers has drawn up a Code of Ethics for panel members which may be a helpful point of reference, on this and other matters.

Statement of Principles

1   The guardian shall maintain independence in all aspects of her work.

2   The guardian shall act in the child's best interests.

3   The guardian shall be committed to bring to court the best evidential base on which decisions must be made.

4   The guardian shall accord value to the child's individuality and shall be concerned to enhance his wellbeing without prejudice.

5   The guardian shall approach every individual without prejudice.

6   The guardian shall be willing to communicate fully about her role, function and value base.

7   The guardian shall search for the means of providing the best and most realistic outcome for the child.

8   The guardian shall conduct her work expeditiously.

Chapter 12

The Best Interests of The Child

DETERMINING A CHILD'S BEST INTERESTS

Two basic points should be made about the best interests of children:

Firstly, as Brenda Hoggett said in her book 'Parents and Children" 'any child whose future has to be decided in litigation has already been deprived of his best interest". What we are looking for is the least "detrimental alternative" as defined in 'Beyond the best interests of the child' (Freud, Goldstein and Solnit 1973;).

Secondly, it must be stressed that there is no one formula or course of action which can guarantee a child's best interests. "What is best for a particular child is indeterminate and speculative and is not demonstrable by scientific proof but is instead a matter of values" (Mnookin and Szwed 1983).

An interesting piece of research, (Phillips 1971) showed that "welfare professionals of similar experience agreed in 50% of cases and even then they did not identify the same factors as influential in their decisions"! It is perfectly possible for a group of professionals to sit round a case conference table, all espousing a commitment to the plan which will be best for the child while at the same time having very different ideas about what the interpretation of "best interest" will mean in practice. Child care policy and practice is, like many other things, subject to fashion and guardians should be wary of swallowing the current received wisdom whole. There is no one course of action which will guarantee a child's best interests all the time—similarly there is no definition of best interests which can protect all of the children all of the time. We are dealing with a balance of probabilities and no more, and guardians are, among other things, agents of professional balance.

Sometimes "the best interests justification for intervention in children's lives can be inadequate and add professional abuse to the abuse already suffered" (Children's Legal Centre). The Cleveland Inquiry in 1987 highlighted the risk of secondary systems abuse of the child during rescue, in addition to the original primary abuse.

Panel members therefore should be prepared to demonstrate to the courts, through their reports and in their giving of evidence, the process by which they have arrived at their particular interpretation of the child's best interests and this will involve explaining the values inherent in their interpretation and the frame of reference from which they are derived.

Good Enough Parenting

Part of the determination of best interests is based on the guardian's assessment of the care being given to the child. What is "good-enough parenting"? As all parents will freely testify, there is no one course of action or method of parenting which will produce the required result—a healthy, well-adjusted adult functioning to the limit of his potential and at peace with himself and the rest of the world. There is no science of parenting and individual judgements can sometimes be fairly subjective. Furthermore, they can vary from one local authority to another and from one social worker to another, leaving parents somewhat bewildered by what may sometimes be the conflicting standards and requirements of the different professionals involved. The "sweet" syndrome is a good example of this. If a mother takes sweets to a child for a contact visit, she may be criticised for attempting to buy the child's affection. If she neglects to take sweets to the child, the comment is often "She didn't even bring the child any sweets"! What is needed therefore is a sharper identification of best interests with a much more forensic approach to its separate components and a recommendation which will take account of the adult the child is to become, as well as the needs of that child in the short term.

FACTORS AFFECTING THE BEST INTERESTS OF THE CHILD

Specific factors	General factors
The wishes and feelings of the child	Society's expectations
	Public safety
The wishes of the parents/ foster carers	Judicial structure
Natural parents' capacity for change	Local authority child care structure
Acceptable degree of risk Secure Attachments	Resources
Identity	Social worker's own skills/knowledge base
Passage of time	

The specific factors have been discussed in Chapters 7 and 8 ("Working with Children" and "Working with Parents and Carers").

General Factors

Society's expectations

These fluctuate wildly between accusations of social workers' over and under involvement in family life. The Kimberley Carlisle Report said *"Society rightly in our opinion is not prepared to tolerate too heavy handed disruptions to family life and expects careful judgement to be exercised in deciding on the appropriate action to be taken with any particular case"*. Social workers are vulnerable to swings of public opinion, and should take care not to be manipulated into a reactive form of social work practice, which may well run counter to their own well-founded professional judgement. It is however sometimes difficult to keep a fix on an objective assessment of best interests when society's expectations are constantly changing.

Public safety

In certain exceptional situations the individual child's interests may not be paramount. Section 22(6) of the Children Act 1989 qualifies the local authority's duty towards a child if it appears to them that it is necessary for the purpose of protecting members of the public from serious injury. Similarly, under section 22(7) the Secretary of State may, in this context, give directions to a local authority for the purpose of protecting members of the public from serious injury and local authorities shall comply with those directions even though doing so is inconsistent with their other duties under this section of the Act.

Judicial structure

Guardians should be aware that, although the Children Act 1989 moves towards a more inquisitorial model with the introduction of concurrent jurisdiction and the removal of the proof and report stage of care proceedings, nevertheless we are still operating in an adversarially based court. This has sometimes proved a clumsy instrument for determining matters of welfare rather than justice. Indeed, institutionalised ambivalence between the philosophies of justice and welfare have dogged many proceedings in the juvenile court, and confused many professionals about the primary purpose of the court proceedings. Is it about identifying the outcome which will be in the best interests of the child, or arriving at a fair and just decision? The two may be incompatible, and even mutually exclusive. Guardians should be aware of these tensions in presenting their evidence, particularly in cases which involve the committal of the child or young person to secure accommodation.

Local authority child care policies

Each local authority operates to some extent like a city state, each with its own policies, practices, procedures and guidelines. In addition, as the Association of Directors and Social Services stated in their preliminary evidence to the Short Committee (1983) "the number of children in care is significantly affected by the policies and practice adopted by a number of other agencies, education, police, housing, supplementary benefits and magistrates. All of this will have a bearing on local authority planning for the child." The local authority is a fragmented parent and collective responsibility for children may peter out at the elected member's level, rather than devolving to one particular person at one particular time. In this situation the best interests of a specific child may become obscured by the needs of the majority.

Resources

It is an uncomfortable fact that social deprivation in all its manifestations renders families vulnerable to losing their children. The Short Report acknowledged the links between poverty and reception into care and pointed out that children in care come disproportionately from geographical areas of high social deprivation. Guardians therefore should be aware of what resources have been committed by local authorities to support children in need and should also be aware that many problems are exacerbated by shortage of resources, particularly in relation to preventative work with families although the requirement of local authorities to provide preventative services has been strengthened considerably under Part III of the Children Act (Local Authority Support for Children and Families). There are, however, profound political and moral issues about the manner and extent of state intervention into family life, particularly of the poor.

Social workers' own values, skills and knowledge base

Guardians should be aware of the frame of reference from which they have derived their own view and interpretation of the best interests of children and should be prepared to have that view scrutinised by the court. Guardians, like everyone else, have their own experiences both of childhood and of bringing up children, and should be sure that their professional judgements are based soundly on well-validated research and professional experience and knowledge, rather than on paediatric mythology. Guardians need to see the child, not just in isolation, but in relation to all aspects of the environmental norm in which he lives.

THE "MINIMUM INTERVENTION TEST" (section 1(5))

Guardians must be satisfied that making an order in relation to a child will be better than making no order at all. To make this judgement they should be aware (if this is a proposed course) of what the care experience is likely to be for the particular child and weigh that against the likely harm of remaining where he is.

A summary of recent research findings (Patterns and Outcomes in Child Placement HMSO 1991) found that children and young people coming into care were already disadvantaged by:

— broken families;

— poor housing and over-crowding;

— poverty;

— unemployment;

— problems of health or disability.

In general, before the 1989 Act, far less attention was given to what was to happen after admission to care than to whether or not the orders should have been made. Research findings indicate that social work attention fades the longer children are in care and that, once in care, many unplanned changes of placement (and social workers) may be experienced. "Periods in public care have further impaired the life chances of some young people because of poor educational achievement, uncorrected health problems and maladjustment" (Kahan 1989 Jackson 1987). Bamford and Wolkind concluded in 1988 that those who had been in care were gravely disadvantaged as a group, with higher risks of psychiatric ill health and social deviance than any other easily identifiable group in society.

Short-term admissions to care can be of great support in relieving family stress, but unless resources are put into the family quickly and the child's early return secured, then the chances of the child remaining in care long-term increase dramatically. Guardians, in common with all social work planners, should be familiar with the appropriate research evidence and outcomes and should be prepared to ask searching questions about what "care" is likely to mean for this particular child. All care provision—short-term, medium and long-term fostering and residential provision can be successful if carefully matched to meet the needs of the child concerned.

CREATIVE PLANNING FOR THE FUTURE

NEGATIVE FACTORS IN THE CHILD'S LIFE	POSITIVE FACTORS IN THE CHILD'S LIFE
Disrupted placements (List all previous carers and placements)	Secure bonds of attachment
Abuse – sexual/physical/emotional	Secure and sustaining contacts with siblings/relatives/friends/teachers
Neglect	Strong sense of identity, race, culture and religion
Disadvantages — poor housing	Any particular skills or aptitudes
Disabilities — e.g. deaf, blind, dyslexic	Good health
Bereavement	Talents — Sports, Art, Music
Loss	Consistent schooling
Grief	Fulfilment of education/physical/emotional potential
Anger	Stable friendships
Juvenile offending	Secure environment
Isolation	Resilience
Insecure attachments	Particular hobbies
Poor Health	Involvement in planning for the future
Poor Education	HOPE
Fewer contacts with peers	

List the negative and positive factor in the child's life. Check that the recommended plan incorporates as many of the positive features as possible, while attempting to limit the effects of the negatives. Any plan should give the child some hope for the future.

PART IV

ADOPTION PROCEEDINGS

Chapter 13

Changes Introduced by the Children Act 1989

INTRODUCTION

Thoughout Chapters 13 to 15, (apart from in legal quotations), the term 'guardian ad litem' is shortened in the text to 'guardian'. Where the phrase 'parent or guardian' arises this does not mean guardian ad litem.

Adoption law is itself currently under review, but the Children Act 1989 introduces some changes in both law and practice as it relates to adoption and freeing for adoption applications.

Guardians ad litem and reporting officers will continue to be appointed under section 65 of the Adoption Act 1976 in order to protect the interests and welfare of the child. They will also continue to provide an important link between adoption and the rest of children's legislation.

For information on the impact of the Children Act 1989 on adoption law see Children Act Guidance and Regulations Volume 9, "Adoption Issues". There is a discussion of some of these issues in the interdepartmental Review of Adoption Law, Discussion Paper Number One—'The Nature and Effect of Adoption' (paragraph 57) (Department of Health September 1991.) In addition to the documents above, guardians and reporting officers should be familiar with:-

— Section 88 and Schedule 10 (Part 1) of the Children Act 1989— Amendments to Adoption Legislation.

— The Adoption Agencies Regulations (Statutory Instrument 1983 No 1964.)

— The Adoption Court Rules—County and High Court—The Adoption Rules 1984 (Statutory Instrument 1984 No 265.), as amended by the Adoption (Amendment) Rules 1991 Statutory Instrument 1991 No 1880

— Adoption Court Rules—Local Authority Circular LAC (84) 10

— The Magistrates Court Adoption Rules 1984 (Statutory Instrument 1984 No 611)

— The Family Proceedings Courts (Matrimonial Proceedings etc) Rules 1991 SI No 1991.

    Children and Young Persons—Arrangements for Placement of Children (General) Regulations 1991

    LAC Circular 84(2) Freeing and Protecting Children.

Unlike proceedings under the Children Act 1989, a child is not a party in adoption and freeing proceedings, except in the High Court where he is automatically a party. This means that guardians do not routinely have the benefit of legal advice in these proceedings unless they are appointed in the High Court.

THE CHILD'S WELFARE

In all proceedings guardians ad litem and reporting officers should bear in mind the requirement of section 6 of the Adoption Act 1976 that:-

"In reaching any decision relating to the adoption of a child the court or adoption agency shall give first consideration to the need to safeguard and promote the welfare of the child throughout his childhood; and shall, so far as it is practicable ascertain the wishes and feelings of the child regarding the decision and give due consideration to them, having regard to his age and understanding."

CASE MANAGEMENT ROLE

The case management role assigned to the guardian in proceedings under the Children Act 1989 does not apply to adoption and freeing for adoption. However, as a matter of good practice guardians and reporting officers should bear in mind:-

* the factors set out in the welfare check list (S1(3)(a–f)) which may also be relevant in adoption;

* the principle that delay is prejudicial to the child (S.1(2)) in adoption and freeing for adoption which applies in adoption as well as in other proceedings;

* the requirement to consider whether making an order will be better for the child than making no order at all (S.1(5)), which may also be a helpful point to consider in adoption cases.

CHANGES INTRODUCED BY THE CHILDREN ACT

The introduction of section 8 orders in adoption proceedings

These are now to be designated "Family Proceedings". The effect of this is that the court can make Section 8 orders of its own motion at any stage of the adoption proceedings and without the need for a formal application for one of the relevant orders by the parties concerned. This extends the courts powers, compared with Section 14(3) of the 1976 Adoption Act.

Section 8 orders may be made in favour of anyone in respect of any child who is the subject of adoption proceedings.

The court will be able to make section 8 orders as an alternative to adoption, where parental agreement has been withheld. A court can make a residence order in favour of the adopters even though the parents have not agreed to the adoption and the court has not dispensed with their agreement.

Abolition of Custodianship Orders.

The power to make custodianship orders is repealed. Instead the court may make a residence order which settles the arrangements to be made as to the person with whom a child is to live. Where the residence order is made in favour of someone who is not the child's parent or guardian, that person is given parental responsibility, but the extent of parental responsibility is restricted by section 12(3) Children Act 1989. Under the transitional arrangements custodianship orders are deemed to confer parental responsibility on the holder of the order for as long as the order lasts.

Section 8 contact order in adoption

Contact Orders are the orders which regulate the arrangements requiring the person with whom the child lives, or is to live, to allow the child to visit or otherwise have contact with another person. Contact can include or be linked to indirect contacts, e.g.. telephone calls, Christmas and birthday cards, letters etc. Conditions can be attached to this order which must be adhered to by the person in whose favour the order is made and also by anyone with parental responsibility for that child.

Contact orders can be made in addition to an adoption order. For example, a contact order could be made in favour of the birth mother or father in a step-parent adoption or a contact order could be made in favour of grandparents or between separated siblings. The court may make a contact order at the same time as freeing a child for adoption.

The Adoption Contact Register

The Children Act 1989 Schedule 10, paragraph 21, introduces the Adoption Contact Register—"The Registrar General shall maintain, at the General Register Office, a Register to be called The Adoption Contact Register".

The Adoption Contact Register is very similar to the Birth-link register already established in Scotland and came into force in England and Wales on May 1st 1991. A series of five booklets have been produced jointly by the Office of Population Censuses and Surveys and the Department of Health. These deal with the Adoption Contact Register, obtaining access to birth records and providing advice to counsellors. They are reproduced in full in the Children Act Guidance and Regulations, Volume 9.

The Register is in two parts—one for adoptees and one for relatives. Through the register information can be stored so that relatives as well as birth mothers and fathers are able to register interest in a particular child in a safe and confidential manner. The decision about whether or not to establish contact is left to the adoptee.

Counselling

There is no requirement for counselling in section 51(A) unlike section 51. However, counselling is available from local authorities under section 1 of the 1976 Act. Several voluntary organisations with experience in adoption counselling (e.g. The Post Adoption Centre, Natural Parents Support Group and NORCAP), have also agreed to provide advice and counselling services for the purposes of the register and to provide an intermediary service for natural relatives who prefer to register an address other than their own, through which the adopted person can make contact. Guardians and reporting officers should ensure that both children and families understand the use of the Register.

There is a provision under Schedule 10 paragraph 20(8) for an adopted person living outside the United Kingdom who wishes to seek access to his birth records to obtain counselling overseas.

Concurrent Jurisdiction in Family Proceedings

Adoption and the new section 8 applications may now be heard at the same time, by the same court. This is a considerable improvement on the former situation where for example an adoption application was made to the County Court and a simultaneous application may have been made by the parents for the Juvenile Court to hear access applications.

"First" or "paramount" consideration?

Under the Children Act 1989 courts are directed, under section 1(1) to give paramount consideration to the welfare of the child. Adoption legislation is different in that it directs the courts to give first consideration to the welfare of the child, but not paramount consideration. One reason for this is to cover the situation where it may be thought to be in the best interests of the child to be adopted but there are no grounds for dispensing with parental agreement where this is withheld.

Adoption applications

The new provisions introduce a limited relaxation on the age limit which prevented adoption applications from anyone under the age of 21. Section 14 of the Adoption Act 1976 as amended allows a step parent and a spouse who is the natural parent of the child to apply for an adoption order where the natural parent of the child is at least eighteen years of age and the step parent at least twenty one.

Freeing Orders

An adoption agency can apply for a freeing order without the consent of a parent or guardian only where the agency is a local authority in whose care the child is by virtue of a care order.

Other points to note in relation to freeing applications are:

* a freeing order does not end any duty to make payments in respect of the child's maintenance or upbringing arising by virtue of an agreement that constitutes a trust or which expressly provides that the duty is not extinguished by the making of an adoption order.

* when making a freeing order courts must be satisfied that a father who has no parental responsibility has no intention of applying either for a parental responsibility order, or a Section 8 residence order or that if he did make such application it would be likely to be refused.

* where the court varies a freeing order to transfer parental responsibility from one adoption agency to another, the new agency will assume all the responsibilities of the adoption agency including progress reports to former parents from the date of the original freeing order.

Unmarried fathers

The Children Act 1989 at section 4 makes it easier for unmarried fathers to acquire parental responsibility. Where this is done, the Court would have to seek their agreement to adoption or, if grounds exist, dispense with such agreement.

IMPLICATIONS:CONTACT ORDERS

The Children Act gives courts powers in adoption proceedings to make section 8 orders on application or of the court's own volition. Courts can therefore make a contact order regulating arrangements for contact, whether physical access or more limited contact, between the adopted child and a member of his or her birth family. In considering the implications of this power, it must be remembered that courts have previously had powers to attach conditions to adoption orders, including, if the court wished, conditions about access and contact. There is, therefore, little substantive change in this respect. Courts have, however, been reluctant to impose such conditions except where all parties, including the adoptive parents, have agreed. Adoption orders with access conditions have been rare and it cannot be assumed that the courts will now take a different view. On the other hand, as adoptions of older children have increased, it has become more common for such children to retain after adoption some limited contact with siblings or grandparents or, more rarely, birth parents. This does not always require an order of the court, where there is agreement and good will on all sides. Some agencies with experience of adoptions with continuing contact point out that such arrangements can call for frequent review and variation as the adopted child matures and becomes securely settled in the adoptive family. The wishes of the child and of others involved may change.

Guardians should continue to investigate and report on the degree of contact between the child and parents and other family members; on the consideration given by the agency to the question of continuing contact; on the agency's views and proposals; and on the views and wishes of the child, prospective adopters and the child's family. There will always, of course, be cases where contact is not desired by any of the parties and cases where contact would clearly not be in a child's interests. But as the Children Act takes effect, with its new provisions in relation to contact where children are looked after; its presumption of reasonable access and its philosophy of partnership between local authority and parents, guardians may find fewer cases where contact has been terminated before the adoption application. More children may reach the stage of an adoption hearing while still in contact with members of their families. Agencies and guardians will need to consider with the child, adopters and birth family the future of these relationships and the implications for any future contact.

The new provisions hold out the possibility of less conflict in adoption proceedings and a much more flexible adoption order, one which can incorporate and accept the child's past as well as offering permanence for the future. Fears that continuing contacts with birth parents and extended family will impede the making of new secure attachments and undermine future security and happiness have proved ill founded in many cases.

Chapter 14

The Role of the Guardian ad Litem in Adoption and Freeing Proceedings

APPOINTMENT AND DUTIES OF THE GUARDIAN AD LITEM IN ADOPTION PROCEEDINGS

These are dealt with at Rule 18, the Magistrates' Court (Adoption) Rules 1984 as amended by the Magistrates' Courts Family Proceedings Courts (Matrimonial Proceedings etc) Rules 1991 (Statutory Instrument 1991).

Appointment

Rule 18 states:

"As soon as practicable after the originating process has been filed or after receipt of the statement of facts supplied under rule 19, if the child is not free for adoption and if it appears that a parent or guardian of the child is unwilling to agree to the making of the adoption order, the proper officer shall appoint a guardian ad litem of the child and shall send to him a copy of the originating process together with any documents attached thereto".

The rule continues:

"Where there are special circumstances and it appears to the court that the welfare of the child requires it, the court may at any time appoint a guardian ad litem of the child, and where such an appointment is made the court shall indicate any particular matters which it requires the guardian ad litem to investigate...".

Rule 18(3) provides that guardians may be appointed as reporting officers and vice versa if the circumstances surrounding the agreement to consent change i.e. if a parent who was formerly willing changes their mind about agreeing to adoption. This means that guardians ad litem and reporting officers should have equivalent qualifications as they may be required to "change hats".

Rule 18(4) states that, in the High Court, unless the applicant desires some other person to act as guardian ad litem, the Official Solicitor shall if he consents, be appointed as the guardian ad litem of the child.

Rule 18(5) provides for the appointment of the guardian ad litem in the High Court if *"the Official Solicitor does not consent to act as guardian ad litem or the applicant desires some other person so to act."*

Duties

Rule 18(6) states that, *"with a view to safeguarding the interests of the child before the court the guardian ad litem shall, so far as is reasonably practicable:*

a.   *investigate:-*

i.   *so far as he considers necessary, the matters alleged in the originating process, any report supplied under Rule 22(1) or (2), and where appropriate, the statement of facts supplied under Rule 19;*

ii.   any other matters which appear to him to be relevant to the making of the adoption order,

b.   advise whether, in his opinion, the child should be present at the hearing of the process; and

c.   perform such other duties as appear to him necessary, or as the court may direct."

Under "any other matters" guardians should consider the wishes of relevant extended family members and the possible use of Section 8 orders.

Rule 18(7), details the guardian ad litem's duties further by referring back to Rule 6:-

"On completing his investigations a report in writing to the court, drawing attention to any matters which in his opinion, may be of assistance to the court, in considering the application" (Rule 6(7)).

"With a view to obtaining the directions of the court on any matter, the guardian ad litem may at any time make such interim report to the court as appears to him to be necessary" (Rule 6(8)).

"The court may, at any time before the final determination of the application require the guardian ad litem to perform such further duties as the court considers necessary" (Rule 6(9)).

"The guardian ad Litem shall attend any hearing of the application unless the court otherwise orders" (Rule 6(10)).

"Any report made to the court shall be confidential" (Rule 6(11)).

APPOINTMENT AND DUTIES OF THE GUARDIAN AD LITEM IN FREEING FOR ADOPTION APPLICATIONS

Rule 6 of the Adoption Court Rules deals with the appointment and duties of the guardian in freeing for adoption applications. These are substantially the same as for the guardian ad litem in adoption proceedings.

There are some additional considerations for practice:

*   Although prospective adopters of a child who is the subject of a 'freeing' application are not parties to the proceedings, it may nevertheless be desirable for the guardian ad litem to interview them.

*   The guardian should where possible, ascertain the position regarding an application for a residence order or parental responsibility by the father of a child (where he was not married to the mother at the time of the child's birth).

*   the guardian should also look at whether the child is likely to be placed for adoption. If this appears unlikely, for one reason or another, then the guardian should look very carefully at the freeing application. Would being 'freed' weaken or strengthen the child's position in relation to achieving permanence of placement?

The Task of the Guardian ad Litem in Adoption and Freeing Applications

Because adoption proceedings are now Family Proceedings, guardians in adoption and freeing proceedings should bear in mind in making their report's recommendations the wider range of orders which will be available to the court. Guardians will naturally be cautious about disturbing a settled and happy situation. They should, however, report to the court on whether the option being recommended (e.g—the adoption order) appears to be the one most likely to secure the welfare of the child in the light of a full consideration of all the relevant alternatives, including the menu of section 8 orders available.

Checklist of the Guardian's Duties: these are in relation to the child, the court, the applicants, the birth parents and the adoption agency:

(This is intended to be a baseline on which to work and not an exhaustive or prescriptive list).

Guardians should not start their investigations until they have received the Schedule 2 report, and other documentation.

The child

* Will the adoption or freeing order be in the best interests of this particular child?

* What are the needs of this particular child including needs in relation to race, culture, religion, language and education?

* What are the wishes and feelings of the child (if of sufficient age and understanding) regarding the application?

* Is the child aware of the application and the circumstances surrounding (if of sufficient age and understanding) and has any necessary counselling been carried out by the adoption agency?

* The guardian will be expected to advise the court about whether or not the child should attend the hearing, and this should be decided in consultation with the child.

* If it appears to the guardian that the child should be a party to the proceedings, ask the court to consider transferring the case to the High Court.

The court

(Remember there will normally be no solicitor)

* Investigate the circumstances surrounding the application.

* Investigate any particular matters as directed by the court.

* Receive and check relevant documents.

* Bring to the attention of the court at an early stage any material matters which have a bearing on the case.

* Interview relevant people including the child, the applicants, the birth parents, and other extended family members if appropriate.

* Make an early decision about the need for expert evidence and inform the court.

* Be prepared to inform and advise the court on existing contact arrangements.

* Request a hearing for directions if necessary.

* Inspect all relevant records.

* Prepare a report and lodge it with the court two weeks before the final hearing.

* Think through how you are going to represent the child, bearing in mind your ability to address the court on the question of whether an adoption order should be made (Rule 23(1)). The assumption is that the child will attend unless there are special circumstances.

The applicants

* Will they meet the needs of this particular child and provide a permanent home for him? This should include consideration of race, culture, religion, language and educational needs.

* Have they received appropriate counselling and support from the adoption agency in making their application?

* Are they aware of the existence and purpose of the Adoption Contact Register? What is their attitude towards contact (if appropriate) by the birth family, including siblings in view of the fact that many more children will arrive at this point with continuing links with their families?

The birth parents

* Why are they withholding their agreement to the making of the adoption or freeing order?

* What is their plan for the child?

* Are they (or any other person with parental responsibility) likely to make an application for any of the orders available under the Children Act 1989, either in private or public law proceedings?

* Have the birth parents received appropriate counselling from the adoption agency and are they aware of the existence and purpose of the Adoption Contact Register?

* What are the existing contact arrangements if any? Is there any problem either in frequency, type or arrangements for contact? If contact exists is it reasonable. Remember that contact may include indirect contacts via birthday cards, letters, and telephone calls.

The adoption agency

* Has the agency fulfilled its duties under the Adoption Agencies Regulations 1983?

* Is the Schedule 2 report available, accurate, and complete? Does it tally with the information on the file, and that given to the adoption panel?

* Has the adoption agency counselled

    — the child

    — the birth parents

    — the applicants

    (as required by regulations 7 and 8—the Adoption Agencies Regulations 1983)?

Has the agency carried out its other specific duties in relation to them i.e. obtaining medical reports and references for the applicants? Has the agency provided information to the applicants as required by regulation 12?

* Is an adoption or freeing for adoption order the best order for this child at this stage in its life?

* Are the particular prospective adoptive parents suitable for this child? Do they meet the child's racial, cultural, religious and linguistic needs?

* Has the adoption agency considered the question of contact?

* Would the order mean that the child lost touch with siblings, particularly those with whom there has been contact?

* Has information been provided to the child, the birth parents and the applicants about the Adoption Contact Register?

Additional Points in Relation to Freeing Applications

* Have the birth parents made a declaration under section 18(6) of the Adoption Act 1976 i.e. Do they wish to be informed of the child's situation and any proposed adoption?

* Does the child (if of an age and understanding) wish the order to be made?

* What are the longer term implications of making the freeing order? What are the realistic expectations of making a suitable placement if the child is freed? What are the agency's proposals? Have prospective adopters been identified? If not, does this child have any special needs which may make adoption more or less likely?

* What are the arrangements for contact with siblings (if any) and the wider extended family?

ADOPTION—POLICY AND PRACTICE

The Adoption Order

An adoption order shall not be made unless the child is free for adoption by virtue of an order made in England and Wales (or the equivalent provision in Scotland) or in the case of each parent or guardian of the child the court is satisfied that:

> *"i.   he freely, and with full understanding of what is involved, agrees unconditionally to the making of an adoption order (whether or not he knows the identity of the applicants); or*
>
> *ii   his agreement to the making of the adoption order should be dispensed with on a ground specified* Adoption Act 1976, section 16(2).

The specified grounds for dispensing with agreement are that the parent or guardian:

> *"a.   cannot be found or is incapable of giving agreement;*
>
> *b.   is withholding his agreement unreasonably;*
>
> *c. has persistently failed without reasonable cause to discharge his parental responsibility for the child;*
>
> *d.   has abandoned or neglected the child;*
>
> *e.   has persistently ill-treated the child;*
>
> *f.   has seriously ill-treated the child."*

The last ground does not apply unless, because of ill-treatment or for other reasons, the rehabilitation of the child within the household of the parent or guardian is unlikely. Agreement is ineffective if given by the mother less that 6 weeks after the child's birth. See also below under **unreasonable withholding of agreement.**

An adoption order severs the legal relationship between a child and its birth parents and vests parental responsibility in the adoptive parents. It extinguishes all other orders under the Children Act 1989. Adopted children may be re-adopted in which case the adopters may give or withhold agreement. (See sections 12(1) and 39(1) of the Adoption Act 1976)

The Freeing for Adoption Order

A freeing order means that all parental responsibility is vested in the adoption agency in whose favour the order is made—as if the order were an adoption order and the agency were adopters. After the order is made all matters relating to the child are decided by the agency including contact. (See sections 18(5) and 12(2) & (3) of the Adoption Act 1976).

Following the making of a freeing order, an adoption order can be made subsequently without parental agreement being sought and without the appointment of a guardian. If the guardian felt there were particular problems ensuing from this, she should notify the court in her report in relation to the freeing proceedings, and ask the judge to note on the file any issues of concern or the need for a guardian to be appointed in any adoption proceedings.

Parents who consent to a freeing order and sign a declaration under section 18(6) of the Adoption Act 1976, are declaring that:

— they no longer wish to be involved in future questions about the child's adoption;

— they are giving up any entitlement to be informed of the child's progress.

Parents who consent to the freeing order but do not sign a declaration become 'former parents' and are entitled to be informed about the progress of the child and the proposed or actual adoptive placements. The former parent may be in a position to apply for a revocation of the freeing order.

If a child has not been adopted or placed for adoption 12 months after the freeing order is made, the order may be revoked on application to the court by a former parent. This would imply that adoption agencies should inform parents if no adoption order has been made after 12 months.

The Adoption Agency

The duties and responsibilities of the adoption agency are dealt with in the Adoption Agencies Regulations 1983.

An 'adoption agency' may be an approved adoption society or a local authority.

The adoption agency has a number of duties in relation to the child and his parent or guardian, and to prospective adopters. These duties are laid out in Regulations 7 and 8 respectively. They include:

i. providing a counselling service to the child, his parent or guardian and to the prospective adopters;

ii. explaining the legal implications of and procedures in relation to adoption to the child, his parent or guardian and adopters;

iii. providing written information on relevant matters.

Guardians should check the extent to which the adoption agency has kept the natural parents informed of the plans for the child.

The Adoption Panel

Adoption panels must have no fewer than seven and no more than ten members. (Regulation 5). The chair should be experienced in adoption work, and the membership must include a medical adviser as well as representatives of the adoption agency, the social services committee (if the local authority is an adoption agency) and at least two independent members. The panel should have a legal adviser who need not necessarily be a member of the panel. The role of the adoption panel is to recommend a course of action in relation to a particular child, but it is for the adoption agency to make the final decision, although the chair of an adoption panel as an officer of the local authority may have delegated power to make a decision under the regulations.

Protected Children

Under section 32 of the 1976 Adoption Act, a child not placed for adoption by an adoption agency becomes a protected child when notice is given to a local authority of intention to apply for an adoption order. Children who are placed for adoption by an adoption agency are not protected children. Protected children fall generally into the following groups:

* where the applicant is a parent, step parent or relative.

* where the applicant is a private foster parent of the child and the child has not been placed by an agency.

* where the applicant is a local authority foster parent and the child has not been placed by an agency (however, a child looked after by a local authority also continues to be looked after).

* where the applicant has a custodianship order or residence order in respect of the child.

* where a child has been brought from overseas to be adopted in the UK.

The Act imposes on local authorities a broad duty to visit a protected child from time to time, to satisfy themselves as to the well-being of the child and to give such advice as to his care and maintenance as appears to be needed. The Children Act repealed the provisions relating to the removal of protected children from those applying to adopt them. Where necessary to protect a child a local authority can apply for an Emergency Protection Order. The Children Act also provides for protected status to come to an end if no application for an order has been made within two years of notice under section 22.

Step-parent Adoptions

The largest group of protected children are those who are the subject of adoption applications by step-parents.

It is of course natural that step-parents wish to feel that they have a 'proper family, all with the same status and surname. All of this can provide children with additional security. It is important, however, to take into account issues related both to the child's identity and to the child's wishes and feelings in the matter. Also to be considered is the child's legal relationship, which an adoption order will sever, with the "other parent" and other relatives on one side of his family. There is therefore a need to consider carefully and discuss with applicants (and the child) whether a residence order would not be a better alternative.

In 1975 it was thought that custodianship would be an acceptably secure alternative to adoption. In practice custodianship has not been as widely used as anticipated in 1975, and it remains to be seen how the section 8 residence orders will be viewed. One disadvantage is that a residence order normally ceases at 16. It is likely that step-parents will still see adoption as the preferred option, as it continues to 18. Acceptance of the possibilities of the new order and the benefits likely to accrue to the child will require careful and sensitive explanation.

(For background reading on this matter, guardians should refer to the report of the Houghton Committee and to literature available from the British Agencies for Adoption and Fostering. Also of relevance is the Inter-Departmental Review of Adoption Law: Discussion Paper 3 'The Adoption Process' 1991).

INTER COUNTRY ADOPTIONS

Guardians may be appointed from time to time in cases involving a child who has been brought from overseas for adoption. These are non-agency placements, but are generally not illegal provided the placement is made outside the jurisdiction and the child is brought into the UK by at least one of the adopters. The child is a protected child and the local authority is required to provide a Schedule 2 report to the court. Both local authorities and guardians must expect to be confronted with particular difficulties in some cases in investigating and collecting information about the background to the adoption.

Guardians are advised to read Department of Health Chief Inspector guidance CI(90)2, CI(90)17 and CI(91)14 and Home Office leaflet RON 117 for background information about intercountry adoption and the policy and procedure which apply when UK nationals wish to adopt a child from overseas.

The information in this section of the Manual is correct at the time of issue. Guardians should be alert for developments and changes in relation to intercountry adoption. Guardians should keep up to date with guidance issued to local authorities and other adoption agencies. These will in future also be sent to managers of GALRO panels for information.

Guardians will find that children brought to the UK for adoption fall into two groups: those who have been granted prior Entry Clearance under the Home Office procedures and those where the applicants have failed to comply with these requirements. These children may have been granted temporary admission or Leave to Enter at a port of entry or may have been brought into the country illegally.

In both groups, guardians may find children who are the subject of adoption applications by relatives as well as non-relatives. Some children will have been adopted overseas, although the adoptions may not be recognised under UK law. (See below for adoption orders which are recognised in the UK).

Children who Enter the UK with Prior Entry Clearance

The task of the local authority in preparing a Schedule 2 report and the task of the guardian is considerably eased where the proper procedures have been observed. Local authorities will have been involved in these cases and carried out an assessment of the adopters' suitability as adopters and made a recommendation to the Department of Health before authorisation by the Home Office of the child's entry. The Department of Health will have been satisfied, so far as possible, that the following documentary evidence has been supplied:

* an account of the reasons for the proposed adoption; evidence of the child's identity and as much information about his circumstances, history and background as can be discovered: this may be a welfare report or similar provided by the authorities in the child' s country of origin or an interview with the parents conducted by a British Embassy of High Commission official.

* evidence that the child is legally available for adoption and that the appropriate authorities support the adoption plans and have authorised the child's departure from the country of origin for the purposes of adoption.

* *either* a valid parental agreement, in a form which would be acceptable to a UK court, i.e., in accordance with Rules of Court (form 7 of the Adoption Rules 1984), given freely and with full understanding of the effects of a UK adoption order, *or* official certification that the child has been genuinely abandoned and the parents cannot be found.

*   a health report on the child on the BAAF Intercountry Adoption Medical Form and that;

*   the Department of Health are satisfied that the prospective adopters can be recommended as suitable adopters for the child, on consideration of a report and recommendation on their suitability by their social services department and of the available information on the child.

On the basis of the information on the child and prospective adopters, the Department of Health will have made a recommendation to the Home Office, (with whom responsibility lies for deciding whether or not a child should be admitted) that, as far as can be judged, the proposed adoption would be in the child's best interests and that the Department have found no *prima facie* reason why a court in the UK would not make an adoption order. These judgements are made with great care, but they are, of course, made on the basis of information available before the child comes to the UK. They cannot prejudice any judgement made by a local authority or guardian in the light of investigation, supervision and observation of the placement in practice or any decision of the courts.

Children who Enter the UK without prior Entry Clearance

In these cases, documentation relating to the circumstances of the adoption, child's history and parental agreement is likely to be restricted to that produced by the applicants. Guardians should examine the Schedule 2 report and other local authority records where appropriate, to establish what the local authority have learned and the extent and validity of the available evidence. Particular attention should be paid to the following:

*   who arranged the adoption? Which intermediaries were involved and how were the applicants put in touch with them? Is it claimed that any *bone fide* welfare organisations were involved and if so, what documentary evidence is available?

*   why did the applicants fail to comply with the Entry Clearance requirements, which are designed to safeguard the interests of children in intercountry adoption?

*   is there reliable evidence of the child's identity? If it is claimed that the child is a foundling, is documentary evidence from the proper authorities available?

*   has parental agreement to the adoption been given? All documents relating to parental agreement should be carefully scrutinised. Is there any cause for doubt about the identity of the person who has signed the agreement or the person who witnessed the signature?

*   similarly, if the court is to be asked to dispense with parental agreement, any evidence of abandonment should be carefully scrutinised.

*   a careful assessment of any possible breach of adoption legislation; applicants should, for instance, be carefully questioned about payments made in connection with the adoption, (including payments to lawyers in the country of origin), bearing in mind the provisions of Section 57 of the 1976 Act (prohibition of certain payments).

Some guardians have written to British Embassies and High Commissions with questions in relation to individual cases and requests for local investigations. The Foreign and Commonwealth Office advise that this practice should cease, as diplomatic posts generally do not have the resources to deal with these enquiries. They cannot, for example, recommend particular lawyers to applicants, or comment on the bone fides of lawyers as intermediaries for adoption. Embassies and High Commissions routinely supply lists of local lawyers (and other services) on request, but this is not a recommendation. In nearly all cases, prospective adopters using lawyers or other intermediaries to find them a child obtain the names of the contacts from other adopters or from information networks in the UK. Nor can overseas posts be expected to locate parents and find out whether parental agreement has been properly given.

The advice above is not intended to discourage guardians from making the fullest enquiries possible. Guardians should address their queries to the Department of Health in the first instance. In some cases the Department may have information about conditions in the relevant country. In others, advice will be sought from the Foreign and Commonwealth Office about the possibility of referring to posts overseas for general enquiries, e.g. of adoption law and procedures, to be made of the responsible authorities. Where this procedure has already been followed by the local authority, guardians may take it that any enquiries which are possible have been made.

In these cases, applicants will rarely have been assessed as prospective adopters by an adoption agency. In many cases, applicants will have obtained a home study report from a private social worker. There are cases where applicants have been refused a favourable recommendation by a local authority because they could not be considered suitable, and have subsequently obtained a favourable report and recommendation from a private social worker and brought a child into the UK outside the Entry Clearance procedures. Other cases which guardians may encounter include those where the assessment process has begun but applicants have refused to complete the process and have gone overseas to obtain a child who is then brought in outside the procedures.

Local authorities who are thus presented with a *fait accompli* face particular difficulties in collecting information about the circumstances of the adoption and in forming a view about what will be in the child's best interests. Authorities may sometimes find themselves having to balance serious doubts about the suitability of the applicants and the placement with their assessment of the relationship which has developed between the child and the applicants. It is important that Schedule 2 reports address these difficulties and draw to the court's attention, fully and frankly, any concerns and doubts felt by the authority. Authorities should not feel that they have no opportunity to influence events or outcomes but should, where necessary, consider the range of options available where there are doubts about the suitability of adopters or about the placement. They should not assume that the only alternative to adoption by the applicants will be that the child will be 'sent back'. Guardians, for their part, should ensure that difficult questions have not been skated over because of the unsatisfactory circumstances of the case, but are analysed and exposed to the court. Regarding the background of the child and the placement, reports should not be restricted to a record of the applicant's account of events without scrutiny, questioning and comment.

Immigration and Nationality Issues

Guardians should ensure that local authorities have investigated the immigration status of the child. Children who are admitted with prior Entry Clearance, i.e., where the Entry Clearance requirements have been fully complied with, are admitted to the UK normally for 12 months in the first instance. An extension of leave will normally be granted at the end of that period if adoption proceedings are under way. If an adoption order is made by a court in the UK, the child will automatically become a British Citizen, provided that at least one of the adopters is a British Citizen.

Children who do not have prior entry clearance but are identified by Immigration Officers at a Port of Entry may be refused admission and returned to their own country straight away, but in practice will normally be granted temporary admission pending further enquiries. There are also children who are not presented to the Immigration Officer and are therefore illegal entrants. Such cases should be reported to the Home Office Immigration and Nationality Department so that the child's immigration status can be regularised. Guardians who are in any doubt about a child's immigration or nationality status should seek advice from the Immigration and Nationality Department of the Home Office.

Overseas Adoption Orders which are Recognised under UK Law

Guardians may occasionally encounter cases where applicants have adopted a child overseas in a country whose adoption orders are recognised under UK statutory law. These are by and large those listed in the Adoption (Designation of Overseas Adoptions) Order 1973. No further adoption order is needed in these cases but adopters may apply for an adoption order in the UK because the child would acquire British nationality thereby. Applicants should be strongly advised to apply instead for the child to be registered as a British citizen. If applicants persist in their wish to apply for an adoption order, the facts should be reported to the court and directions sought.

OTHER GENERAL ISSUES WITH RESPECT TO ADOPTION AND FREEING APPLICATIONS

Appeals

A guardian has no right of appeal in adoption and freeing proceedings. If the child is a party to the proceedings, an appeal may be lodged on behalf of the child. If an appeal is lodged by one of the parties the guardian stays with the case, and her report would be submitted to the court hearing the appeal.

Interim Adoption Orders

Under section 25 the court on an application for an adoption order has at its discretion the power to make an interim order for a probationary period of not more than two years. The question of parental agreement must have been settled and the local authority duly notified in accordance with section 22 in the case of a non-agency placement. A subsequent hearing is still necessary to determine whether a full adoption order should be made.

Conditions

Adoption Orders may be made with such conditions attached as the Court thinks fit (section 12). Courts have said that such conditions are not to be inconsistent with the concept of adoption as a transfer of parental responsibility i.e. they must not interfere with the adopters' exercise of their responsibility. This again is a rarely used provision which, before the introduction of the new section 8 orders, did give courts the opportunity to order access or other contact as a condition.

Accommodated Children

Freeing orders cannot be made in respect of children accommodated by local authorities unless the parents agree. If grounds for a care order existed, the local authority might consider this course and then apply to free the child.

The Rights of Children

Guardians should note that children who are made the subject of an adoption order, may come to court to seek or vary a section 8 order.

Confidentiality

Applicants who wish to preserve the confidentiality of their identity may ask the Court to allocate a Serial Number which should then be used in all documents likely to be seen by the birth family (Rule 14). These include the guardian's report. Under the rules only the reporting officer and guardian, if appointed, are to be served with a copy of the application form, background report supplied to the court (in freeing cases) and Schedule 2 report. However, parties who are individuals, usually both parents or prospective adopters, referred to in a report supplied to the court may inspect or be supplied with a copy or any part of a report which refers to them, subject to any directions from the court. The court may direct that the individual is not to be shown the report, or that it is only to be shown to his or her legal advisers or that the whole report should be shown to the individual. It is therefore suggested that report writers ensure sections of their report are on separate pages, to facilitate the showing of relevant points without risking a breach of confidentiality in respect of the remainder of the report.

Prospective applicants should be alerted to the need to complete NHS Form FP58B (revised) in order to ensure that the birth parents cannot trace the child by asking for a lost medical card. The Register is not amended until this form has been received even if the child has already been registered with a general practitioner.

Sensitive Material

If there are any matters in the guardian's report which are of particular sensitivity, these should be highlighted in a covering letter to the court, or by drawing them to the attention of the court at an early stage as appropriate.

After the Hearing

If the adoption order is made, the guardian should ensure, as a final task, that the child understands the implications of the order made and the reasons why the court made the decision. If there are matters of policy which are a matter for concern these may be identified in the report and raised separately with the adoption agency.

Unreasonable Withholding of Agreement

There are six grounds for dispensing with parental agreement. These are set out in section 16 of the Adoption Act 1976 as amended by the Children Act 1989 and are reproduced earlier in this chapter.

The grounds and their use, together with relevant case law are examined in the 'Inter-Departmental Review of Adoption Law'. Discussion Paper Number 2 Agreement and Freeing (Department of Health September 1991). Guardians who may need to investigate the statement on which the applicant will rely in asking the court to dispense with parental agreement on the grounds of unreasonableness, will find this publication of particular relevance.

Report Format of the Guardian ad Litem in Adoption or Freeing Proceedings

This format is intended to be used as a basis on which to work—it is not intended to be exclusive or prescriptive!

In general, the guardian's report in adoption or freeing proceedings will be shorter than those in care and related proceedings, and should avoid unnecessary repetition without neglecting to point out any inaccuracies or omissions in the information provided. The key task is the checking of the information not the reproduction of it. As the guardian's report is in part a commentary in the Schedule 2 report (where that is appropriate), it may be counterproductive for the guardian to commence visits until the report has been received.

Under the court rules the primary responsibility for supplying the court with the necessary background information with regard to the child, prospective adopters and birth family rests with the adoption agency or local authority. Since the guardian is only involved in contested or unusual cases her responsibility is to fulfil the specific duties under the rules and comment on any inaccuracies or inadequacies revealed in the Schedule 2 report.

1.　　Front sheet

(Reports should not be typed on agency headed notepaper. They should be marked confidential with numbered paragraphs)

Name of Guardian ad Litem

Date of appointment

Date of Hearing (if known)

Court

Name(s) of the child/children or Serial Number

Date(s) of birth (age)

2.　　Second section

Date on which the child was placed with the applicants (in adoption proceedings) OR

Details of the child's current placement with dates of placement (in freeing proceedings).

Family structure (list members of the birth and extended family with dates of birth and any other relevant information).

— "In preparing this report I have interviewed the following people" (list everyone interviewed, with dates, number of occasions seen, relationship to the child/children).

— "I have spoken to the following on the telephone" (name, relationship, date).

— "I have attempted to interview the following, but have not succeeded for the following reasons" (if relevant).

— "I have seen the following documents" (the adoption agency file, the Schedule 2 Report, witness statements, photographs and medical reports etc).

— A brief summary of earlier hearings (give details of earlier hearings and their outcomes, together with the dates and reasons for any earlier adjournments).

— A statement of any special matter the guardian may wish to bring to the attention of the court (for example, if you have particular concern about the availability of counselling to the relinquishing parent or the position of a child who is the subject of a freeing application).

— A brief statement of the matter before the court and the circumstances surrounding it e.g.. "This child is the subject of an adoption application. He has been with the applicants for five years and the birth mother is withholding her consent to the adoption".

3. Third section

Headings:

(Provided that the guardian is satisfied with the information in the Schedule 2 Report, these sections may be fairly brief to avoid unnecessary repetition, and be confined to expanding on or correcting any errors in the Schedule 2 report, in addition to adding any relevant information acquired in the preparation of the report).

1. **Brief chronological history of the case and a summary of the relevant facts,** including placement information with dates, the present status of the child (i.e.. in care, in accommodation, a protected child etc), any existing contact arrangements, with details of the practical arrangements attached to them, i.e.. the form the contact takes, visits, telephone calls, birthday cards.

2. **The child**. Details of the child's race, culture, disabilities, religion and languages understood or spoken, both by the child and those who have cared for him. Details of health and education, hobbies, likes, dislikes etc.

3. **The birth family,** their reasons for either giving or withholding consent to the proposed adoption or freeing application, their attitude to the proposed adoption or freeing application and their wishes in respect of continuing contact with the child;

4. **The applicants.** A brief statement of their involvement and commitment to the child, with particular attention to their suitability as adoptive parents to meet the needs of this particular child. This section should take into consideration the child's race, culture and religion in assessing the suitability of the applicants as adoptive parents. The guardian should also look at the child's physical, emotional and educational needs and the capacity of the applicants to meet them adequately. Guardians should be sensitive to the position of the adoptive parents, and may wish to interview them, possibly before seeing the child, in order to establish the child's state of knowledge about the proceedings.

5. **The wishes and feelings of the child.** This section should be clearly and separately identified. In particular, the guardian should seek to determine the child's wishes in relation to the proposed adoption, and identify any alternatives that the child would consider desirable, if appropriate. Include the child's views on existing or continuing contacts with the birth family (if appropriate). This section should not contain the guardian's own interpretations or opinions about the stated wishes and feelings of the child, which should come later as part of the guardian's assessment and recommendation.

6. **The work of the adoption agency in planning for this particular child.** Guardians will be looking at the adoption agency policies and practices and the work carried out, both with the relinquishing family and the applicants and the child, as outlined in the Schedule 2 report and the adoption file.

7. **The impact of delay**—Comments which the guardian wishes to make about the timetabling of the case and the likely impact on the child. The Schedule II report for example should be with the Court within six weeks of notification of a hearing date (LAC (84)10 Paragraph 56).

8. **The relevant options available to the court.** Bearing in mind the range of Section 8 Orders now available to the court in adoption proceedings, the guardian should address the following two issues. Firstly, is an adoption order the best way to meet the needs of this particular child? Secondly (if the parents are withholding their agreement to the adoption), why are the parents refusing to agree to the adoption order?

9.   **The guardian's assessment.** This should include the assessment of the child's present situation and a statement of whether or not the order sought, or any other, might be most appropriate to meet the needs of this particular child. It should also include an assessment of the advantages and disadvantages of both direct and indirect contact. The guardian should address the issue of whether or not the birth parents and the child have been offered adequate counselling services by the adoption agency.

10. **Recommendation.** The guardian's recommendation should be clear, with a brief statement of why the she considers that the recommendation is the one which will best serve the interests of the child. As the Guardian ad litem in Adoption and Freeing proceedings comes in to the child's life at a fairly late stage, the recommendations should look to the child's future and what will be best, taking into account all the circumstances of the case.

Chapter 15

The Role of the Reporting Officer in Adoption and Freeing Applications

APPOINTMENT AND DUTIES OF THE REPORTING OFFICER IN ADOPTION PROCEEDINGS

These are to be found in Rule 17 and Rule 5 of the Magistrates' Courts Rules 1984 amended by the Magistrates' Courts Family Proceedings Courts (Matrimonial Proceedings etc) Rules 1991.

Appointment

"As soon as practicable after the originating process has been filed or at any stage thereafter, if the child is not free for adoption and if it appears that a parent or guardian of the child is willing to agree to the making of an adoption order and is in England and Wales, the proper officer shall appoint a reporting officer in respect of that parent or guardian, and shall send to him a copy of the originating process, and any documents attached there to." Rule 17(1)

"The same person may be appointed as reporting officer in respect of two or more parents or guardians of the child." Rule 17(2)

"The reporting officer shall be appointed from a panel of guardians ad litem and reporting officers and should not have been "involved in the making of any arrangements for the adoption of the child." Rule 17(3)

Duties

Rule 17(4) states that the reporting officer shall:

"a.   ensure so far as in reasonably practicable that any agreement to the making of the adoption order is given freely and unconditionally and with a full understanding of what is involved;

b.   witness the signature by the parent or guardian of the written agreement to the making of the adoption order;

c.   investigate all the circumstances relevant to that agreement; and

d.   on completing his investigations make a report in writing to the court drawing attention to any matters which, in his opinion, may be of assistance to the court in considering the application."

Rule 5 sets out further duties of the reporting officer, namely:

"With a view to obtaining the directions of the court on any matter, the reporting officer may at any time make such interim report to the court as appears to him to be necessary and, in particular the reporting officer shall make a report if a parent or guardian is unwilling to agree to the making of an adoption order, and in such a case the proper officer shall notify the applicant." Rule 5(5)

"The court may, at any time before the final determination of the application require the reporting officer to perform such further duties as the court considers necessary." (Rule 5(6))

"The reporting officer shall attend any hearing of the application if so required by the court." (Rule 5(7))

"Any report made to the court under this rule shall be confidential." (Rule 5(8))

APPOINTMENT AND DUTIES OF THE REPORTING OFFICER IN FREEING FOR ADOPTION PROCEEDINGS

Rule 5 deals with the appointment and duties of the reporting officers in freeing for adoption proceedings. The rules are substantially the same as those for the reporting officer in adoption proceedings, with two additions:-

Rule 5(4)(b)—requires the reporting officer to:

> *"confirm that the parent or guardian has been given an opportunity of making a declaration (under Section 18(6) of the Adoption Act 1976) that he prefers not to be involved in future questions concerning the adoption of the child."*

Rule 5(4)(e) states that where it is proposed to free an illegitimate child for adoption and his father is not his guardian then the reporting officer should interview any person claiming to be the father in order to be able to advise the court regarding the father's intention or non-intention of applying for any of the orders available to him under the Children Act 1989.

The Task of the Reporting Officer in Adoption and Freeing Proceedings

Essentially the task of reporting officer is to protect the rights of the birth parents by ensuring that the agreement to the adoption or freeing order is given:

*   unconditionally

*   freely

*   with full understanding of the nature and effect of the order.

While the task is limited in scope it is nevertheless extremely important and may in practice be very complex. It requires the same level of experience and expertise as that required of guardians. Indeed, the two roles are designed to be interchangeable. Rule 5(3) states that reporting officers must be appointed from a panel local to the parent rather than the court. In addition, the reporting officer must bring to the court's attention any matter which may give cause for concern about a case, indicating the need for a further investigation. In certain circumstances a reporting officer may be re-appointed to the case, but as a guardian. This might well arise if there is concern about the welfare of the child or if there are doubts that the agreement of a parent is given freely, unconditionally and with full understanding.

A summary of tasks includes:

*   receive documentation and return Form 16.

*   read the Schedule 2 Report to gain an understanding of the salient features of the case;

*   ensure that the agreement to adoption or freeing for adoption is given freely and with full understanding;

*   ensure that parent understands application process to make a declaration under section 14(7).

*   check that the parent understands the existence and function of the Adoption Contact Register.

*   witness the signature of the willing parent to the child's adoption or freeing for adoption;

* investigate all circumstances relevant to the giving of the consent, including whether or not adequate counselling has been made available to the relinquishing parent;

* request additional information from the Schedule 2 Report writer, and discuss whether more work is needed in the light of any circumstances revealed by the interview with the relinquishing parent;

* write a report for the court;

* carry out any other duties which the court may direct.

See also LAC (84)10 paragraphs 9–16 and 49–50.

In freeing applications the reporting officer should note that:

* conditions may not be attached to a freeing order, unlike an adoption order.

* the adoption panel should have considered the effects of making a freeing application before an application is made to the court.

* the adoption agency must provide the court with a statement of facts giving the sequence of events which have led to the freeing application being made.

* the adoption agency has a duty to have regard as 'far as practicable' to the parents wishes regarding the child's religious upbringing. They do not have a similar duty to have regard to the child's race and culture in making a placement (section 7 Adoption Act 1976). Agencies are, however, expected as a matter of good practice to have regard to a child's needs arising from his racial origin and cultural background and there expectations are set out in departmental guidance (CI(90)2).

Step-parent Adoptions

A birth parent who is adopting their only child with that child's step-parent must also give their agreement and sign Form 7. Reporting officers should check that the implications of the change in their legal status in relation to their child and the implications for the child's legal relationships with existing family members and the step-parent's family members is clearly understood. Similarly, guardians should ensure that birth parents who are willing to agree to adoption by a step parent understand these issues. Reporting officers should check that the relevant persons understand the concept of parental responsibility and how it applies to the application.

Documents

The reporting officer should receive from the court:

> The completed application form
> One or two blank copies of agreement Form 7
> The child's birth certificate
> The Schedule 2 report (may arrive separately)
> Notice of hearing
> Health Reports where applicable
> Notice of Reporting Officer appointment and acknowledgement of documents form 16—*to be completed and returned immediately.*

Before visiting the parent the reporting officer should wait to receive the documents and the Schedule 2 Report from the court. If there appears to be undue delay in its arrival the reporting officer should seek directions from the court. There may be exceptional circumstances in which it would be appropriate for the reporting officer to commence enquiries without waiting; for example, if the birth parent whose consent is sought is shortly to leave the country.

Withdrawal of Agreement

The reporting officer should make sure the parents understand the implications of adoption or freeing and should inform them that, although they have signed the consent form, they may withdraw their agreement up to the time the adoption order is made. It should, however, be made clear that if parents do this, their position may be prejudiced if a long period has elapsed and the child has had the opportunity to settle with the prospective adopters. Once agreement has been given to the making of an adoption order and an application for adoption has been made (or an application for a freeing order has been made without agreement) the child cannot be removed without the leave of the court.

The reporting officer should also ask the parent to identify their child's birth certificate by signing the back of it.

If there are contact issues which are not fully resolved, and especially if there are indications that the child may have views about the loss or continuation of contact with the birth family the reporting officer should notify the court or request the appointment of a guardian ad litem.

Adoption Contact Register

Reporting officers should ensure that the parents know they have the right to register or lodge information on the Adoption Contact Register and should explain the implications of the adopted child's access to their birth record and to the contents of the Adoption Contact Register at the age of eighteen.

Reporting Officers should beware of diminishing the finality of the adoption order in the eyes of the relinquishing parent or placing undue emphasis of the likelihood of children attempting to trace their birth parents once they achieve adulthood. It would be wrong for parents to assume that this will be the likely outcome.

Report to the Court

The reporting officer's report will be concise, outling the actions of the reporting officer and any areas of concern about the Schedule 2 report. There should also be:

* a brief statement of the circumstances in which the agreement has been given;

* confirmation of the parents' understanding of the implications of adoption;

* confirmation that information about the existence and function of the Adoption Contact Register has been given;

* in freeing applications—whether or not the relinquishing parent has made a declaration;

* a statement of any other matters which the reporting officer feels it is appropriate to bring to the attention of the court.

APPENDIX 1

Summary of the Sections of the Children Act 1989 of Direct Relevance to Guardians ad Litem and Reporting Officers

Over-riding principles

Section 1(1)   The welfare of the child is of paramount consideration in all decision making

Section 1(2)   Delay is prejudicial to the child

Section 1(3)   The welfare check-list

Section 1(5)   The principle of minimum intervention. No order should be made unless the court is satisfied that the likely outcome for the child of making the order will be better than making no order at all

Orders

Section 8 orders:

— Residence;

— Contact;

— Prohibited steps;

— Specific issue.

(Section 11(7)   allows the attachment of directions and conditions to section 8 orders)

Section 16   Family Assistance Orders

Section 25   Secure Accommodation Orders

Section 31   Care Orders and Supervision Orders;

Section 36   Education Supervision Orders;

Section 43   Child Assessment Orders;

Section 44   Emergency Protection Orders;

Section 50   Recovery Orders—recovery of abducted or missing children;

Major Provisions

Section 17   Local authority services to children and families

Section 17(10)   Deals with children in need of those services. a child is said to be in need if:

> (a)   *he is unlikely to achieve or maintain, or have the opportunity of achieving or maintaining, a reasonable standard of health or development without provision of services by a local authority under this Part [i.e., Part 3 of the Act];*

(b)   his health or development is likely to be significantly impaired or further impaired, without the provision for him of such services; or

(c)   he is disabled

NB. "Development" in this context means physical, intellectual, emotional, social and behavioural. A child is considered disabled if he is blind, deaf or dumb or suffers mental disorder of any kind or is substantially and permanently handicapped by illness, injury or congenital deformity (section 17(11))

Section 20   Children provided with accommodation (NB No notice of removal required))

Section 22   The *welfare principle* which underlies all local authority decision making. This section includes a direction to the local authority to give due consideration to the child's religious persuasion, racial origin, cultural and linguistic background, as well as to the child's wishes and feelings and to the wishes and feelings of key people in the child's life.

Sections 22(3), 26(1)   General welfare duties placed on local authorities, including duty to carry out reviews to plan for the welfare of the child

Secti ↑ 24   Leaving care provisions

Section 23(6)   Order of priority for choosing possible foster parent i.e. if not parents then relatives, friends, other persons connected with the child

Section 23(7) (a) and (b)   Children to be placed near the family home and with siblings if at all possible

Schedule 2, paragraphs 15 and 16   Promotion of contact between child and family and friends

Section 27   Co-operation between different local authorities and departments within local authorities to enable children and families to receive appropriate services, e.g. co-operation with housing and education departments

Schedule 2, paragraph 10   Maintenance of the family home:

"Every local authority shall take such steps as are reasonably practicable, where any child within their area who is in need is and whom they are not looking after is living apart from his family -

(a) to enable him to live with his family; or

(b) to promote contact between him and his family, if, in their opinion, it is necessary to do so in order to safeguard or promote his welfare."

Section 34   Presumption of reasonable contact with parents, siblings and extended family

Section 34(6)   Local authority may refuse reasonable contact if:

"(a)   they are satisfied that it is necessary to do so in order to safeguard or promote the child's welfare; and

(b)   the refusal—

  (i) is decided upon as a matter of urgency;

  (ii) does not last for more than 7 days."

Guardian ad Litem and Reporting Officer provisions

Section 41   Appointment of Guardians ad Litem—Powers and Duties

Section 42   Guardian ad Litem's access to records

Miscellaneous Provisions

Section 32(1)   Drawing up a timetable and avoiding delay

Section 88 and Schedule 10   Amendment to Adoption provisions

Section 96   Allows children to give unsworn evidence in certain circumstances

Section 100(4)   Wardship provisions

APPENDIX 1

APPENDIX 2
Copy of Order making or refusing the appointment of a Guardian ad Litem Form CHA 30

In the
at

[High Court of Justice]
[County Court]
[Magistrates' Court]

———————— The Children Act ————————

Order making or refusing the appointment
of a Guardian ad litem

Case No.

Section 41(1) The Children Act 1989

———————— The Children Act ————————

| 1 | The child is a [boy] [girl] born on |

| 2 | The court orders that [*   ] (a guardian ad litem) be appointed for the child *Insert name of guardian ad litem if known* |

| 3 | [An appointment is not necessary to safeguard the interests of the child] |

| 4 | The proceedings to which this order relates are |

☐ application for care or supervision order

☐ directions or interim care order under section 37 or section 38

☐ application for discharge of care order

☐ application for variation or discharge of supervision order

☐ application for substitution of supervision order for care order

☐ consideration of residence order for a child in care

☐ contact/refusal of contact with child in care

☐ other proceedings (specify)

☐ proceedings under section 33(7)

☐ emergency protection order

☐ an appeal

☐ proceedings under section 25

☐ applications under paragraph 19(1) Schedule 2

☐ applications under paragraph 6(3) Schedule 3

☐ child assessment order

———————— The Children Act ————————

This order was made on

[Mr/Mrs Justice]
[His/Her Honour Judge]
[District Judge [of the Family Division]]
[Justice of the Peace]
[Clerk of the Court]

———————— The Children Act ————————

APPENDIX 3

Copy of Annex from The Care of Children "Principles and Practice in Regulations and Guidance"

(*To avoid tedious repetition, the terms "children" and "young people" are used interchangeably and either or both should be assumed to cover the whole age range 0–18 years).

(1)   *Children and young people and their parents should all be considered as individuals with particular needs and potentialities.*

(2)   *Although some basic needs are universal, there can be a variety of ways of meeting them.*

(3)   *Children are entitled to protection from neglect, abuse and exploitation.*

(4)   *A child's age, sex, health, personality, race, culture and life experience are all relevant to any consideration of needs and vulnerability and have to be taken into account when planning or providing help.*

(5)   *There are unique advantages for children in experiencing normal family life in their own birth family and every effort should be made to preserve the child's home and family links.*

(6)   *Parents are individuals with needs of their own.*

(7)   *The development of a working partnership with parents is usually the most effective route to providing supplementary or substitute care for their children.*

(8)   *Admission to public care by virtue of a compulsory order is itself a risk to be balanced against others. So also is the accommodation of a child by a local authority.*

(9)   *If young people cannot remain at home, placement with relatives or friends should be explored before other forms of placement are considered.*

(10)   *If young people have to live apart from their family of origin, both they and their parents should be helped to consider alternatives and contribute to the making of an informed choice about the most appropriate form of care.*

(11)   *When out-of-home care is necessary, active steps should be taken to ensure speedy return home.*

(12)   *Parents should be expected and enabled to retain their responsibilities and to remain as closely involved as is consistent with their child's welfare, even if that child cannot live at home either temporarily or permanently.*

(13)   *Siblings should not be separated when in care or when being looked after under voluntary arrangements unless this is part of a well thought out plan based on each child's needs.*

(14)   *Family links should be actively maintained through visits and other forms of contact. Both parents are important even if one of them is no longer in the family home and fathers should not be overlooked or marginalised.*

(15)   *Wider families matter as well as parents—especially siblings and grandparents.*

(16)   *Continuity of relationships is important, and attachments should be respected, sustained and developed.*

(17)   *Change of home, caregiver, social worker or school almost always carries some risk to a child's development and welfare.*

(18) *Time is a crucial element in child care and should be reckoned in days and months rather than years.*

(19) *Every young person needs to develop a secure sense of personal identity and all those with parental or caring responsibilities have a duty to offer encouragement and support in this task.*

(20) *All children need to develop self confidence and a sense of self worth, so alongside the development of identity and equally important, is self esteem.*

(21) *Since discrimination of all kinds is an everyday reality in many children's lives, every effort must be made to ensure that agency services and practices do not reflect or reinforce it.*

(22) *Corporate parenting is not "good enough" on its own.*

(23) *Young people should not be disadvantaged or stigmatised by action taken on their behalf, e.g. as a result of admission to care or to special residential provision.*

(24) *Children's long-term welfare must be protected by prompt, positive and pro-active attention to the health and education of those in both short and long-term care.*

(25) *Young people's wishes must be elicited and taken seriously.*

(26) *As young people grow up, preparation for independence is a necessary and important part of the parental role which child care agencies carry for young people in long-term care.*

(27) *In carrying out the duties and responsibilities laid upon them in the legislation and regulations, local authorities should put into practice the principles of good work with children and families which are set out in the previous section.*

(28) *The various departments of a local authority (e.g. health, housing, education and social services) should co-operate to provide an integrated service and range of resources even when such co-operation is not specifically required by law.*

(29) *The twin issues of confidentiality and access to records need to be addressed by all local authorities and child care organisations.*

(30) *Caregivers are entitled to have appropriate information about any child or young person placed in their charge and have a duty to keep this confidential.*

(31) *Letters and documents which are sent to parents and young people should be written in language which is fully comprehensible to them.*

(32) *Planning is a crucial responsibility for all agencies providing services to children and their families.*

(33) *Agencies have special, parental responsibilities for the minority of children who are in long-term out-of-home placements.*

(34) *When alternatives are being considered and/or decisions made, certain individuals or groups may need to be involved.*

(35) *Services to vulnerable children have to be largely provided through those who give them day to day care whether these are parents, relatives, residential social workers or foster carers. In each case, a balance must be struck between offering carers support (thus building confidence) and holding them accountable for the child's well-being.*

(36) *Caregivers—whether parents, foster carers or residential staff—need both practical resources and a feeling of being valued if they are to give of their best.*

(37) *Appropriate training should be provided for carers.*

(38) There should be machinery for resolving differences of view or minor disputes, e.g. through involvement of a team leader, fostering officer or other appropriate individual or through renegotiating written agreements at the request of any of the signatories.

(39) Agencies have a responsibility to support placements which they have made.

(40) Registers and records must be maintained and kept up to date.

(41) Co-operation between organisations, departments and individuals is crucial in the provision of protection for vulnerable children and also in ensuring proper use of available resources.

(42) Foster homes and residential establishments used for the placement of children should be reviewed at regular and suitable intervals though this needs to be done sensitively so as to avoid undermining carers' confidence or making children feel insecure.

PART II

APPENDIX 4

Case Study

The following case study illustrates some of the possibilities of the new legislation:

ANNA

Anna is six. Since her parents' divorce she lives with her mother, Sheila aged 22, and her mother's co-habitee, Bill aged 31. He has two children by a previous marriage and a criminal record of robbery with violence. Four months ago Anna was referred to the Social Services Department by the school, who reported that she was pale, listless and apathetic and that twice she had appeared at school with minor bruising about the face. Two months ago she was put on the Child Protection Register. Now she has told a trusted teacher that Bill is sexually abusing her. The school notified the Social Services Department who held a case conference and applied for an Emergency Protection Order. Sheila is sent for and arrives at school shocked and unwilling to believe Anna's story. Anna is placed in a short term foster home. Sheila sees a solicitor and says that she will apply for the discharge of the Order as soon as possible, i.e. after 72 hours.

The Court alerts the guardian ad litem through the duty system. The guardian ad litem now has 48 hours left in which to form an opinion about whether or not to support the application to discharge the Emergency Protection Order.

What does the guardian ad litem do now?

1.   Appoints a solicitor from the Child Care Panel.

2.   Contacts the local authority social worker and checks the social services file to see what information is available.

3.   Interviews Sheila and Bill, both together and separately, in their own home.

4.   Interviews Anna's teacher.

5.   Visits Anna to: (a) reassure her;

(b) explain what is happening;

(c) ascertain her wishes and feelings.

6.   Asks Anna who she would like to see (if anybody). This may be a teacher or school friend, as well as a parent or relative.

7.   Checks on contact arrangements.

The guardian ad litem now knows:

1. That Anna wants to see her mother, but is frightened of Bill. She therefore checks the arrangements for contact with Sheila during the period of the Emergency Protection Order.

2. Sheila will not co-operate, either in asking Bill to leave the home so that Anna can return, or in taking steps to remove him. She doesn't believe Anna's story and says that she has always been a "little troublemaker".

Note. Sheila could have applied to the County Court for a short term Ouster Injunction under section 1 of the Domestic Violence and Matrimonial Proceedings Act 1976 or (if Sheila and Bill had been married) for an Exclusion Order under section 16 of the Domestic Proceedings and Magistrates Court Act 1978.

3. Anna used to be close to her paternal grandmother before her parents divorced but hasn't seen her for six months, since Sheila began living with Bill. Anna's father, John, is working abroad on oil rigs but sees her when he returns home at three monthly intervals. Anna tells the guardian that her paternal grandmother still writes to her regularly but is not made welcome at the house by Sheila and Bill.

The guardian ad litem traces the grandmother and visits her the same day. She finds her very upset to hear what has happened and immediately asks to have Anna with her. She is a widow of 55 with adequate accommodation for her grand-daughter. She says that if she could only have Anna with her, Sheila would be welcome to visit her whenever she liked.

The guardian ad litem confers with the local authority social worker, who asks Sheila if she would agree to Anna undergoing a period of assessment, during which time she could stay with her paternal grandmother. Sheila refuses to enter into any voluntary arrangements with the local authority. At the hearing, the local authority withdraws its application for an Emergency Protection Order and applies for a seven day Child Assessment Order. The guardian ad litem supports this application.

In making the Order the Family Proceedings Court directs that Anna should live with her grandmother for the duration of the seven day Order, during which time she can have unlimited contact with her mother. The Court also directs that the Assessment Order should include a medical examination. The guardian ad litem talks to Anna about this and explains what is involved. Anna is fearful of the examination and the guardian ad litem makes it clear that she can refuse the examination if she wishes. However she agrees, after:

 (a) being reassured that her grandmother can be present throughout; and

(b) being given a clear explanation of what is involved.

[This raises the question of whether a 6 year old may be judged to be competent to make such a decision, and whether it is possible to give competency at a particular age.]

After seven days the Child Assessment Order expires and the parties return to Court.

1. The medical examination supports Anna's allegation of sexual abuse.

2. Sheila still refuses to believe Anna and will not agree to Anna remaining with her grandmother.

3. Bill will not leave the house.

The local authority have held a case conference and now believe they have grounds for a Care Order. They consider it would be unsafe to return Anna to her mother's home while Bill is there. Sheila will not protect her and does not believe Anna's story and Bill is unwilling to leave. Anna is happy with her grandma but Sheila won't agree to her staying there, so no voluntary arrangement is possible. The local authority are concerned about Anna's long term situation. Grandma has a pacemaker and the additional stress of looking after Anna may affect her health. Sheila is not taking advantage of the contact visits, even though the local authority has given help with fares and taxis to see Anna (section 17(6)). The local authority social worker thinks Anna should be placed in long-term foster care, with continuing contact with mother and grandmother. They therefore apply for a Care Order under section 31 and the guardian ad litem is reappointed for those proceedings.

Meanwhile grandma sees a solicitor and decides to apply for a section 8 Residence Order and the Police decide to pursue criminal proceedings against Bill for his offence against Anna. Both the care and residence order applications can be heard in the Magistrates Family Proceedings Court, but the guardian could have asked for the case to be transferred to the County or High Court on the basis of the transfer criteria or to another Magistrates Court if no court time was available in the area (section 41.10 — Guardians ad litem responsibility for allocation and time-tabling of cases). In the meantime an Interim Care Order has been made for twenty-eight days, unopposed by the child's solicitor or the guardian ad litem. During that period the guardian ad litem advises the court that contact with Sheila should continue but that Bill should not be allowed to see Anna. The local authority agree to Anna remaining with the grandmother for the period of the twenty-eight day order.

Bill's solicitor tries to postpone the care proceedings until after the outcome of the criminal proceedings, saying that the outcome may prejudice his client's case. The court and the guardian invoke their powers under section 3(2) avoiding delay to ensure that the care proceedings are heard within 12 weeks of the original Emergency Protection Order.

At the final hearing the guardian ad litem opposes the making of a Care Order for the following reasons:

(a)   although the grounds for the making of a Care Order are proved, she does not believe that making a Care Order will be the best order in the circumstances. If the guardian had considered that a Care order was the best order she would still have to consider section 3(5) whether making an order was better than making no order at all.

(b)   there is a viable alternative home with grandma, who is now supported in her application for a Residence Order by Anna's father, John, who has been seen by the guardian ad litem and, although not able to offer Anna a permanent home, has agreed to spent more time with her and his mother in order to offer support.

(c)   Anna is desperate to stay with her grandmother and not go to live with strangers.

The local authority are now prepared to withdraw their application for Care Order but are still worried about Bill having access to Anna through Sheila. They consider applying for an Interim Supervision Order in conjunction with a section 8 Residence Order to monitor the situation with grandma and Anna but decide that this will not be necessary.

The Court makes a section 8 Residence Order in favour of the paternal grandmother, who then acquires parental responsibility, and a section 8 Prohibited Steps Order prohibiting Bill to have any further contact with Anna whatsoever. This last order covers the possibility of Bill being found "not guilty" or not receiving a custodial sentence. The Court was able to make a Prohibited Steps Order although technically Bill was not a person with parental responsibility because the Order covers any steps which could be taken by a parent in meeting his parental responsibility of a kind specified in the Order whoever that person is i.e. it is the step that is prohibited not the person. If the court had not accepted this the guardian could have considered applying to have the case transferred to the High Court which could have been asked by the guardian to exercise its inherent jurisdiction under section 100 to make an anti-molestation injunction to keep Bill away from Anna.

It is important to note that, although the threshold criteria for the making of a section 31 Care Order were satisfied in this case, it is not necessary to satisfy the criteria in order to make any section 8 Order.

Additional Points

1. The idea behind section 8 Orders is that the legislation should provide a framework which can be adapted to suit the child's situation, rather than the child having to adapt to the limitations of the legislation.

2. In looking at the possibility of making a residence order, guardians ad litem should bear in mind that the order will normally cease when the child is sixteen. This was one of the weaknesses of the old custodianship order. Children do not leave home physically, emotionally and financially on their sixteenth birthday and the fact that the order ceases at sixteen could be seen as a weakness in terms of providing a statutory framework for continuing support of the child during the vulnerable years between sixteen and twenty-one.

3. Throughout the period of the guardian's involvement she will be liaising with the Court regarding:

(a) timetabling of the case and the avoidance of harmful delay (section 1(2));

(b) giving the court early warning of any likely holdups;

(c) making sure that the practical arrangements for the case to be heard have been made i.e. Is there a court available with enough court time to hear the case on consecutive days;

(d) checking with the Justices Clerk that all parties are aware of the arrangements and are ready to proceed;

(e) requesting any Directions Hearings necessary;

(f) alerting the court to any party's failure to carry out the court's instructions re contact;

(g) reasonable contact.;

APPENDIX 5

Essential and Recommended Reading for Guardians ad Litem and Reporting Officers

Guardians ad litem should read, and should have access to copies of:

The Children Act 1989, as amended by the Courts and Legal Services Act 1990 and the NHS and Community Care Act 1990.

The Adoption Act 1976

The Family Proceedings Courts (Children Act 1989) Rules 1991 Part II

High Court and County Court Rules Part IV

The Guardian ad Litem and Reporting Officers (Panels) Regulations 1991

An Introduction to the Children Act 1989—A new framework for the care and upbringing of children—HMSO 1989

The Children Act 1989 Guidance and Regulations Volume 1—Court Orders (HMSO 1991)

The Children Act 1989 Guidance and Regulations Volume 2—Family Support, Day Care and Educational Provision for Young Children (HMSO 1991)

The Children Act 1989 Guidance and Regulations Volume 3—Family Placements (HMSO 1991)

The Children Act 1989 (Guidance and Regulations Volume 4—Residential Care

The Children Act 1989 Guidance and Regulations Volume 5—Independent Schools (HMSO 1991)

The Children Act 1989 Guidance and Regulations Volume 6—Children With Disabilities (HMSO 1991)

The Children Act 1989 Guidance and Regulations Volume 7—Guardians ad Litem and other Court-Related Issues (HMSO 1991)

The Children Act 1989 Guidance and Regulations Volume 8—Private Fostering and Miscellaneous (HMSO 1991)

The Children Act 1989 Guidance and Regulations Volume 9—Adoption Issues (HMSO 1991)

Child Abuse—A Study of Inquiry Reports 1980 to 1989 (HMSO 1991)

The Care of Children—Principles and Practice in Regulations and Guidance (HMSO 1989)

Child Care Policy—Putting it in Writing—A Review of English Local Authority Child Care Policy Statements (HMSO 1990)

Patterns and Outcomes in Child Placement—Messages from current research and their implications (HMSO 1991)

Looking After Children: Assessing Outcomes in Child Care (HMSO 1991)

Significant Harm: its Management and outcome Ed. Margaret Adcock, Richard White & Anne Hollows (Significant Publications 1991)

In the Interests of Children—An Inspection of the Guardian ad Litem and Reporting Officer Service (Social Services Inspectorate 1990)

The Report of the Inquiry into Child Abuse in Cleveland 1987 (HMSO 1988)

Working Together—A Guide to Arrangements for Inter-agency Co-operation and the Protection of Children from Abuse (HMSO 1991)

Protecting Children—A Guide for social workers undertaking a comprehensive assessment (HMSO 1988)

The Pindown Experience and The Protection of Children—The Report of the Staffordshire Child Care Inquiry 1990—Published by Staffordshire County Council 1991.

Children and Young Persons—Review of Children's Cases Regulations 1991 (Statutory Instrument No 895)

Children and Young Persons—Arrangements for Placement of Children (General) Regulations 1991 (Statutory Instrument No 890)

Children and Young Persons—Representations Procedure (Children) Regulations 1991 (Statutory Instrument No 894)

Children and Young Persons—Placement of Children with Parents etc Regulations 1991 (Statutory Instrument No 893)

Children and Young Persons—The Foster Placement (Children) Regulations 1991 (Statutory Instrument No 910)

Children and Young Persons—The Children (Representations, Placements and Reviews) (Miscellaneous Amendments) Regulations 1991 (Statutory Instrument No 2033)

Children and Young Persons—Inspection of Premises, Children and Records (Independent Schools) Regulations 1991 (Statutory Instrument No 975)

Children and Young Persons—Contact with Children Regulations 1991 (Statutory Instrument No 891)

Children and Young Persons—Definition of Independent Visitors (Children) Regulations 1991 (Statutory Instrument No 892)

Children and Young Persons—Children's Homes Regulations 1991 (Statutory Instrument No 1506)

Children and Young Persons—Children (Secure Accommodation) Regulations 191 (Statutory Instrument No 1505)

Children and Young Persons—Children (Secure Accommodation) (No 2) Regulations 1991 (Statutory Instrument No 2034)

Children and Young Persons—Refuges (Children's Homes and Foster Placements) Regulations 1991 (Statutory Instrument No 1507)

Children and Young Persons—Transfer Orders and Recovery of Children 1991 Statutory Instrument No 2032)

Children and Young Persons—The Emergency Protection Order (Transfer of Responsibilities) Regulations 1991 (Statutory Instrument No 1414)

Children and Young Persons—Child Minding and Day Care (Applications for Registration) Regulations 1991 (Statutory Instrument No 1689)

Children and Young Persons—Child Minding and Day Care (Registration and Fees) Regulations 1991 (Statutory Instrument No 2076)

Children and Young Persons—Disqualification for Caring for Children Regulations 1991 (Statutory Instrument No 2094)

Children and Young Persons—Children (Private Arrangements for Fostering) Regulations 1991 (Statutory Instrument No 2050)

Children and Young Persons—Adoption Allowance Regulations 1991 (Statutory Instrument No 2030)

Children and Young Persons—The Children Act (Commencement and Transitional Provisions) Order 1991 (Statutory Instrument No 828)

Children and Young Persons—The Children Act (Commencement No 2—Amendment and Transitional Provisions) Order 1991 (Statutory Instrument No 1990)

The Children Act 1989—Putting it into Practice (Open University Training Pack)

On Behalf of the Child—The work of the Guardian ad Litem, Anna Kerr, Eva Gregory, Susan Howard and Freda Hudson (Venture Press 1990)

National Association of Guardians ad Litem and Reporting Officers—Code of Ethics for Guardians ad Litem and Reporting Officers and Code of Practice and the Role and Function of Panel Managers (National Association of Guardians ad Litem and Reporting Officers 1991)

The Guardian ad Litem—Law and Practice, Pat Monro and Liz Forrester, Family Law (Jordans 1991)

Time for Me (Communicating with Children), Compiled by Suzette Waterhouse (1987) (available from 34 Bell Lane, Byfield, Northants)

Children In Need and Their Families—a new approach—A Guide to Part 3 of the Children Act 1989 for local authority counsellors, Martin Shaw, Judith Masson and Edwina Brocklesby (University of Leicester and the Department of Health 1990)

Going Into Care—A Talkabout book for social workers for use with their children (Five Rivers Residential Project, Avon House, 28 Windham Road, Salisbury, Wiltshire SP1 3AB (Tel 0722 334138))

Key Issues in Child Sexual Abuse: Some Lessons from Cleveland and other Inquiries, Margaret Richards, National Institute for Social Work (NISW Information Service Briefing Paper)

House of Commons Second Report from the Social Services Committee Children in Care (The Short Report) (HMSO 1984)

Separate Representation for Parents and Children—An examination of the initial phase, Mervyn Murch with Kay Bader (University of Bristol Family Law Research Unit 1985)

Guardian ad litem Reports—a Research analysis, Jim Richards (Available from 73 St Charles Square London W10 6EJ Price £7.50p)

Social Work Decisions in Child Care—Recent Research Findings and their Implications (HMSO 1985)

Courts and Legal Services Act 1990

The NHS and Community Care Act 1990

Child Abuse, Christina Lyon and S P de Ia Cruz (Jordans 1990) Speaking Out for Children—Finding from the Voluntary Sector's first specialist guardian ad litem team, Joan Hunt with Mervyn Murch (The Children's Society 1990)

The Children Act 1989—Training Together, a training and curriculum model for the Children Act 1989 by the Family and Child Care Law Training Group (London November 1989)

A Guide to the Children Act 1989, Richard White, Paul Carr and Nigel Lowe (Butterworths 1990)

Who Cares?—Young People in Care Speak Out, edited by Raissa Page and G A Clarke (National Children's Bureau 1977)

The Implications of the Children Act 1989 on Children and Young People with Severe Learning Difficulties (Barnados and University of Keele 1991)

Safeguarding Children—A Guide to the Work of the Guardian ad Litem in Care Proceedings, Don Clark (from Kenton Sussex ICA Publications, Cherry Tree Cottage, Peasmarsh, Nr Rye, East Sussex TN31 6SP)

Representing Children—Child Interviews—a pictorial aid for guardians ad litem and child care panel solicitors, Don Clark (from Kenton Sussex ICA Publications, Cherry Tree Cottage, Peasmarsh, Nr Rye, East Sussex TN31 6SP)

Living Away from Home—Legal Impact on Children with Severe Learning Difficulties (Barnados and University of Keele 1991)

The Rights and Wrongs of Children, Michael Freeman (Pinter 1983)

Reports—BASW Publications, Guardians/ Curators ad Litem and Reporting Officers (British Association of Social Workers 1986)

Panels of Guardians ad Litem and Reporting Officers, (Joint ADSS/ACC/AMA Officers Working Party Report, February 1986)

The Representation of the Child in Civil Proceedings, Research Project 1985 to 1989, Summary of Conclusions and Recommendations for the Department of Health by Mervyn Murch, Joan Hunt and Alison McLeod (Socio Legal Centre for Family Studies, University of Bristol, January 1990)

Who Says? Choice and Control in Care, Ruth Gardner (National Children's Bureau)

Interpreters in Public Services, Phil Baker with Zahida Hussain and Jane Saunders (Venture Press in association with the Further Education Unit, BASW, 16 Kent Street, Birmingham B5 6RD)

In Care: A Study of Social Work Decision Making, Vernon J and Fruin D (National Children's Bureau 1986)

Child Care General The Needs of Children, Mia Kellman Pringle (Hutchinson 1974)

Perspectives in Child Care Policy, Lorraine M Fox Harding (Longman 1991)

Child Placement—Principles and Practice, June Thoburn (Wildwood House 1988)

Understanding Child Abuse, David N Jones and David Pickett, 2nd Edition (Macmillan Education 1987)

The Politics of Child Abuse, Nigel Parton (Macmillans 1985)

Gaskin, James MacVeigh, (Jonathan Cape Limited 1982) The story of one boy in care

Social Work with Black Children and their Families, Ahmed S, Cheetham J and Small J (Eds) (Batsford 1986)

Sexually Abused Children—Making Their Placements Work, Daphne Batty (ed) (BAAF 1991)

The Evidence of Children—The Law and The Psychology, J R Spencer and Rhoma Flin (Blackstone 1990)

Reports to Courts—Practice Guidance For Social Workers (HMSO 1987)

Professionals and the Courts—A Handbook for Expert Witnesses David Carson. (Venture Press 1990)

Improving Social Work Records and Practice, John Ovretreit (BASW Action Research 1986)

Living with a Mentally Handicapped Child, Judy Jeffard (Social Work Monographs, University of East Anglia, Norwich 1990)

ADOPTION AND FOSTERING

Adoption Act Manual, Richard Jones (Sweet and Maxwell 1988)

Adoption, Margaret Richards (Family Law 1989)

Adoption—Essays in Social Policy Law and Sociology, Philip Bean (ed) (Tavistock Press 1984)

A collection of essays dealing with adoption and social policy, adoption and the law and a topical section on trans- cultural adoption

Adoption Law and Practice, Nasreen Pearce (Fourmat 1991)

Long Term Foster Care, Jane Rowe, Hilary Cain, Marion Hundleby and Ann Keane (Backford Academic and Educational in association with BAAF, 1984)

Hard to Place—The Outcomes of Adoption and Residential Care, Trisoliotis J P and Russell J (Heinemann and Gower 1984)

Children Who Wait, Jane Rowe and Lydia Lambert (ABAFA Publications 1973)

Permanency Planning for Children—Concept and Methods, Malucchio Fein and Olmstoad (Tavistock 1986)

Permanence in Child Care, June Thoburn, Anne Murdock and Alison O'Brien (Blackwell 1986)

Beyond the Best Interests of the Child. Freud, Goldstein and Solnit (Macmillan 1973)

The Permanency Principle in Child Care Social Work, Catriona Morris (Social Work Monographs, University of East Anglia, Norwich) An excellent review of the available research on permanence

Attachment, Separation and Loss (Volumes 1-3), John Bowlby (Penguin Education 1969)

RECOMMENDED PERIODICALS

CHILD RIGHT—Published by Children's Legal Centre, 20 Compton Terrace, London N1 2UN

FAMILY LAW—Published by Jordans, PO Box 260, 21 St Thomas Street, Bristol BS99 7DX

ADOPTION AND FOSTERING—Published by quarterly by BAAF (11 Southwark Street, London SEI IRQ)

JUSTICE OF THE PEACE

PANEL NEWS—Published by IRCHIN, 23A Nawthorne Drive, Heswall, Wirral, Merseyside L61 6UP (Tel 051 342 7852) *A quarterly journal for Guardians ad Litem, Reporting Officers, Child Care Law Solicitors and all those interested in child care law and practice*

SEEN AND HEARD—published by the National Association of Guardians ad Litem and Reporting Officers.
Bi -monthly newsletter for members

CHILDREN AND SOCIETY—a multi-disciplinary Journal published by the National Children's Bureau, Published Whiting and Birch, 90 Dartmouth Road, Forest Hill, London SW19 7BX

THE JOURNAL OF CHILD LAW—published quarterly by Frank Cass & Co Ltd, Gainsborough House, 11 Gainsborough Road, London E11 IRS.

APPENDIX 6

Useful Names and Addresses for Guardians ad Litem and Reporting Officers

ASC — Advice Advocacy and Representation Service for children, 1 Sickle Street, Manchester 2. Free phone Advocacy line for children and young people 0800–616101.

Provides independent support and advocacy services to children and young people. These services are provided both directly and under contract to local authorities and voluntary organisations to assist them in carrying our their statutory duties in relation to children and young people in care.

BAAF (British Agencies for Adoption and Fostering)

11 Southwark Street
London SE1 1RQ
(Telephone 071–407–8800)

BASW (British Association of Social Workers)

16 Kent Street
Birmingham B5 6RD
(Telephone 021–622–3911)

Provides advice and representation services to all its members, including guardians ad litem and reporting officers. Subscription includes weekly copies of Social Work Today

Child Line

0800–1111
24 Hour Help Line for Children

Children's Legal Centre (CLC)

20 Compton Terrace
London N1
(Telephone 071–359–6251)

Department of Health

Community Services Division
Wellington House
133–155 Waterloo Road
London SE1 8UG

IRCHIN (Independent Representation for Children in Need)

Director — Judith Timms
23A Hawthorne Drive
Heswall
Wirral
Merseyside L61 6UP

IRCHIN provides training and an information and advice service for guardians ad li tem and reporting officers, a quarterly journal for panel members (Panel News) and services of consultancy, annual review and training both for new and experienced panel members and other child care law professionals. Subscription £15 annually.

National Association of Guardians ad Litem and Reporting Officers

31 Southern Parade
Frenchwood
PRESTON PRI 4NH
(Telephone 0772–88414 Fax 0772–884229)

Subscription of sixty-five pounds a year includes professional indemnity insurance and bi-monthly copies of the Association's newsletter

NAYPIC (National Association of Young People in Care)

20 Compton Terrace
London N1
(Telephone 071–226–7102)

National Children's Bureau

8 Wakeley Street
London EC1V 7QE

The Adoption Contact Register

The Officer of Population Censuses and Surveys

The Central Register Office
Adoptions Section
Smedley Hydro
Trafalgar Road
Birkdale
Southport PR8 2HH

The Law Society

113 Chancery Lane
London WC2A 1PL
(Telephone 071–242 1222)

The Official Solicitor's Department

Penderal House
287 High Holborn
London WC1V 7HP
(Telephone 071–936–7119)

The Ombudsman

21 Queen Anne's Gate
London SW1H 9BU
(Telephone 071–222–5622)

Voice for the Child in Care (VCC)

Director — Gwen James
15 Wilkin Street

London NW5
(Telephone 071–267–5940)
Provides advice to children in care and in conjunction with ASC.

Who cares? magazine (For children in care)

Editor Tory Laughland
National Children's Bureau
8 Wakley Street
London EC1V 7QE
Provides copies of In Care — Your Guide to Solving Problems. Offers an advice service to children in care and those connected with them.